Judging Architectural Value

HARVARD DESIGN MAGAZINE READERS
William S. Saunders, Editor

Judging Architectural Value

A Harvard Design Magazine Reader

Introduction by Michael Benedikt
William S. Saunders, Editor

University of Minnesota Press | Minneapolis | London

The essays in this book previously appeared in *Harvard Design Magazine,* Harvard University Graduate School of Design; Peter G. Rowe, Dean, 1992–2004; Alan Altshuler, Dean, 2005–.

Thanks to coordinator Meghan Ryan for her work on *Harvard Design Magazine.*

Every effort has been made to obtain permission to reproduce the illustrations in this book. If any acknowledgment has not been included, we encourage copyright holders to notify the publisher.

Published by the University of Minnesota Press
111 Third Avenue South, Suite 290
Minneapolis, MN 55401-2520
http://www.upress.umn.edu

Library of Congress Cataloging-in-Publication Data

Judging architectural value / William S. Saunders, editor ; introduction by Michael Benedikt.
    p.   cm. — (Harvard design magazine readers ; 4)
    Includes bibliographical references.
    ISBN-13: 978-0-8166-5010-1 (hc : alk. paper)
    ISBN-13: 978-0-8166-5011-8 (pb : alk. paper)
    1. Architectural criticism. 2. Architectural design.
  3. Architecture—Philosophy. I. Saunders, William S.
    NA2599.5.J83 2007
    720.1—dc22
                                  2006032375

Printed in the United States of America on acid-free paper

The University of Minnesota is an equal-opportunity educator and employer.

12 11 10 09 08 07   10 9 8 7 6 5 4 3 2 1

Contents

Preface
William S. Saunders

One of the most popular argumentative clichés in this country is "It's all just a matter of opinion." In essence this is laziness—an effort to duck responsibility for having to support and clarify your thoughts. The retreat into subjectivism can, of course, have respectable intellectual foundations: truth is a personal and social construct; claiming to know "reality" is an act of presumption and arrogance. Well, sure. But this is quite different from saying, "I believe this to be true. I cannot be certain, but I can explain why I believe. I am eager to test my beliefs by seriously considering different and contrary beliefs. Perhaps together we can come to agree that one understanding of reality deserves affirmation more than any other, at least until someone convinces us otherwise." The ultimate point may be that none of us can avoid assertions about truth, since every thought we have is implicitly such an assertion (even "there is no truth").

Now, all this becomes trickier and more challenging when the truth being sought is "What is the value and quality of the attempted human achievement before us?" And this is because there are so many and so varied legitimate measures of value, and personal valuations are so much less questionable than personal assertions about empirically measurable "facts." Near me is an old wooden upholstered rocking chair. How good it is can be measured in terms of its durability, its comfort, and the aesthetic quality of its lines and forms. But I like it less than my wife does because my neck hurts when I read in it—personal evaluation can be quite simple.

In the case of architecture (including designed landscapes), as my essay in this volume details, dozens of sometimes contradictory measures of value seem sound, starting from Vitruvius's "firmness, commodity, and delight." Still, we can argue about which values are most important and why, and we can believe that someone else's measures are trivial, shallow, or irrelevant.

The pertinent fact in the context of this book is that nearly every essay written for *Harvard Design Magazine* has been enmeshed in and makes claims about questions of architectural value, intentionally or unintentionally, consciously or unconsciously. The selection of chapters for this volume, covering several years of writing, features those essays that have most self-consciously and carefully explored what makes architecture in general (or more often, in particular) bad, good, and great.

Introduction
Michael Benedikt

To live is to evaluate. To live among others is to *be* evaluated.

Let me elaborate. In order to survive, all living creatures must be able to distinguish the good for themselves from the bad for themselves. Basics are uncomplicated. But by the time evolution yields up human beings living in societies with multiple institutions—science, government, education, the professions, and many others—the processes by which evaluation happens and the targets at which evaluation is aimed become multifarious. Good for *me* becomes tempered by good for *us,* good for *right now* by good *in the long run.* Every action finds itself linked to others in long chains of preconditions, procedures, and protocols, some of which seem to be "only social," others overly painstaking, even superstitious, but most of which, in fact, serve to incorporate ever more information into our decision making. Out of this evolving, ever-complexifying filigree, patterns emerge. Definitions of *value* multiply and compete, not just because what each institution does is different, but because each has an interest in self-perpetuation—indeed, in expansion—under the general mandate of all living species, all institutions, all ideas, to grow, replicate, and proliferate, if necessary at the expense of others.

Architecture is an institution. And like the others, it is crisscrossed by the values put forth by other institutions, even as it seeks to perpetuate and proliferate its own. This is why our wanting to honor an architect, building, style, or model of practice above others in a public way—accepting some values from outside and projecting others into the milieu—is entirely natural. It is also why difficult questions arise, such as by what criteria, internal or external, should honor be bestowed on buildings and their architects? Who shall do the judging and who the bestowing? And let us not forget this question: Who cares? Who *ought* to care?

The essays collected in this fourth Harvard Design Magazine Reader address just such questions. I shall introduce each one and try to stitch them together. To do this, however, I need to offer an analysis of the *venues* in which and the corresponding *values* by which architecture is currently evaluated.

First, there are the venues in which (and the processes through which) architects publicly honor each other: design awards, competition wins, publication in professional magazines and books, election to FAIA status, invitations to lecture at schools of architecture, and so on. In each venue, some sort of jury or editorial review is involved that gives the evaluation a measure of objectivity. The values that dominate are values like significance or uniqueness of program, compositional or formal freshness, mastery of some new technology, fineness of construction, and "narratability" (having the makings of a good story). These values are often disguised by the jargon of the day.

Evaluation of architects and their buildings by the *public,* on the other hand, proceeds in a far more casual manner: publicly in a few newspapers and "dwelling" magazines, privately around watercoolers or in cars driving by new projects, and so on. Here the values of livability, contextuality, "classiness," price, and goodness for the local economy come to the fore, plus simple judgments of ugliness or beauty ("I *like* it." "*I* don't."). The public also expresses its opinion, anonymously and in the aggregate, by its market behavior: the places people like to visit, the "properties" people like to invest in or rent. And it expresses itself through local government: city ordinances, development review processes, neighborhood review boards, and so on, all of which aim to restrain architects' desires to be expressive and experimental, on the one hand, and/or to please a private client, on the other.

Architects are also evaluated by those who *commission* them—I mean clients and their financiers—and these individuals tend to judge architects on yet other bases, such as their friendliness, reliability, efficiency, experience in a certain building type, fees, level of service, signature style, and often mere consanguinity or a social connection. These evaluations are made in other venues: at interviews, around boardroom tables, by word of mouth, at social events, and after tours and site visits.[1]

And finally architects (and their work) are evaluated by members of *allied professions* and occupations. I mean engineers, interior and landscape designers, contractors, suppliers, craftsmen, and so forth. Among these groups—and let's just say this and get it over with—architecture's internal values are an especially hard sell. More important to them is ease of construction and the architect-at-hand's speed, devotion to teamwork, and "flexibility."

Four venues, then, and at least twenty applicable values. So again, whose judgments and whose values should prevail?[2] If the right answer is "a balance of all," then by what means could that balance be achieved? Could/should some authority—perhaps an architecture magazine—arrive at an overall scoring system that publicly evaluates this architect or that building to be superior to others in a *comparative* way? Magazines like *Road & Track* and *Photo* do this for cars and cameras every month. They provide rank orderings and elaborate reasons for every call. Why not *Architecture* architecture?

I shall not go into why my suggestion is not likely to be adopted. But it does raise the question of whether and how the general public's evaluative voice is heard by architects, and of who, exactly, evaluates buildings on its behalf. Is the public's voice heard at all? Citing architects' elitism, some would say, "not enough." Citing the marketplace, others would say, "too much already." In deciding who is more right (for both have a point), it helps to remember why we have *professions* in the first place.

A member of a profession—any profession—is a person who claims the public's *trust* by having received a specialized (and itself accredited) education, having experienced a period of supervised apprenticeship, having passed special examinations, and now holding a state-issued license to practice.[3] Two kinds of trust are fundamental: the trust that the professional will serve the client using the best knowledge available in the field, and the trust that the professional will preserve and promote the public good.[4] Why is either trust needed? The first is needed because in all but the most obvious cases of incompetence, clients are unable to judge the goodness of the service provided. It is simply beyond their training or ability to tell whether they are receiving good, let alone the *best,* service. This is why we permit the surgeon to do what he advises. (Whom do we go to for a second opinion? Another surgeon.) This is why we sign where the accountant says, "sign."

The second trust is needed because the public as a whole simply cannot stay on top of the welter of decisions that daily affect the welfare of all. Moreover, the second kind of trust means that clients can afford to be selfish in what they commission a professional to do. For they can rest assured that the professional is not only *trained* to uphold the public interest (even as they serve theirs) but is also *pledged* to doing so.

Alas, and also happily, no profession today operates quite so insulated from the hurly-burly of the marketplace. At the extreme, clients (and patients) behave like consumers or customers, demanding "value for money," expecting immediate results, and taking their business elsewhere if they are inconvenienced or offended. And many professionals are happy to oblige, behaving rather like competitive on-demand *providers.* To them, refusing service, or advising a client away from their immediate self-interest and toward their longer-term self-interest (or, heaven forbid, the *public* interest) seems presumptuous, elitist, paternalistic, undemocratic, insulting of the intelligence of the client/customer, and so on, and so on—not to mention bad for business.

As antidote, loyalty to a/the profession is salutary. The practitioner's duty to uphold the profession's values and standards *must* discount the public's opinion (and often the last client's opinion too) of the quality of his or her work. Cast into the very DNA of the institution of architecture, as into the DNA of medicine, law, and the other professions, I am pointing out, is a certain indifference to lay criticism.

We can think of this as a good thing. Ordinary people really *do not* know enough. But when the public finds an articulate voice in an educated and popular critic, as it sometimes does, that voice is discounted too, and this may not be a good thing.[5] Members of the public too often suffer their town's Architecture—banal or exotic as the case may be—in silence, shaking their heads at what architects do, and one has to wonder why. Is it their inability to articulate their suffering or even *know* that they are suffering despite the critic's help? Do ordinary people feel insecure about their right to complain about the mediocre and pretentious "junkspace" that constitutes the bulk of our environment? Or is it prudential: is it an unwillingness to ever find themselves persuaded to divert resources from their present pleasures to architectural ones, which are expensive, and which, God forbid, they might come to *need*? I don't know. But I would suggest that opening up nonmarket channels of critical communication between architects and the general public, *going both ways,* has the same urgency in this century that it had in the last.

Two groups remain whose opinion architects care about: other architects (and here I include architecture critics, historians, and writers) and clients. Gathered in this Harvard Design Magazine Reader is a selection of notable articles by the first group.[6] Although it represents only the first of the four "venues" in which architecture is evaluated, what this group thinks, values, and writes matters. It matters at the better architecture offices, which strive always to advance the field as they serve the client and the public good, and at the better architecture schools, where architecture's values are constantly being debated, not just transmitted.

It should not go unnoticed in all this, however, that although the chapters presented here are evaluative of certain architects and their work, they are also implicitly evaluative of each other and of architectural evaluation itself. Historians, critics, editors, and writers in architecture play on a field of contestation too, competing with each other as to the importance of their values, as to the trenchancy of their observations, and as to the effects of their thought upon the practice of the day. And no one is more tempted to evaluate the evaluators than writers of introductions to books like this. I shall try not to abuse the privilege.[7]

Hélène Lipstadt opens this volume with discussion of Eero Saarinen's Gateway Arch in St. Louis, Missouri. We are at once intrigued. Designed in 1948 and completed in 1963 to much public acclaim, the Gateway Arch nonplussed both the sculpture-critic community and the architecture-critic community. Neither an arch nor a gate, neither architecture nor sculpture, what was it exactly? And why, today, is it so rarely taught?

Upon the armature of this elusiveness, Lipstadt offers a distinction that reappears in many of the chapters that follow: that between *icon* and *canon,* iconicity and canonicity. Almost magical in its optical effects, the very uniqueness of the Arch projects it into the realm of iconicity, says Lipstadt. But it cannot function as part of a *canon,* which is to say, as a work judged by most as the best of its kind *and* worthy of being a model for others to follow in rule if not actual form. The Statue of Liberty and the Eiffel Tower are also more iconic than canonic, except that they are typical of landmarks, are good landmarks, and reach poetically upwards. They too are just too unique.

And then there is the sheer popularity of the Arch. "Understanding the *Arch as an icon that is not canonic*," Lipstadt writes (her emphasis), "initiates a special sort of historicization rich in emancipatory potential." Emancipatory? Emancipating us from the style of historical assessment that disvalues popular appeal ipso facto, as against the reigning International Style model championed by Gropius—an architecture designed, as it were, not to need design, only correct carrying out—Saarinen carved a path that led as directly to Venturi as to Gehry. Using sociologist Pierre Bourdieu as her guide, Lipstadt takes the view that "a disdain for iconic buildings is inculcated in architectural education along with . . . a respect for canonic buildings." To do otherwise would be to teach exceptionalism and to allow popular opinion to be the judge of architecture, which is, of course, unprofessional in the terms I offered earlier, not to mention lacking in "class." Lipstadt does not make this argument exactly. But its implication remains. More than a history, Lipstadt's essay is a model of deep investigation into the sociological (i.e., class) and cognitive categorical assumptions that underlie the whole enterprise of architectural criticism.

Given the ecstatic reception of Gehry's iconic buildings today by young architects, the public, and the architectural press, one wonders whether we have become the wiser. Perhaps the difference lies in Gehry's methods and forms, which at least *seem* to be imitable, and thus elevate his later oeuvre to potential canonicity. Or perhaps it is Gehry's mind-set, precedent-set, and client-set, and the constant identification of all three with the art world, high (Bilbao) and low (Experience Music Project in Seattle). How classy—how confusing—is that? It's not Saarinen's world anymore.

And yet one might not think so to judge by the reception of the PSFS building in Philadelphia designed by George Howe and William Lescaze. In "What Goes Unnoticed," David Leatherbarrow makes a case for its canonicity despite, or perhaps because of, that building's Art Deco style (interior and exterior), which, to the present-day eye, seems timelessly elegant, and that building's spatial, structural, and programmatic "ultrapracticality." (This was the term used during its design and that was set before Howe and Lescaze to achieve.)

"Does the identification of a building's style or its formal precedents," Leatherbarrow asks, "help us understand its contemporary and continued importance, in either architectural design or everyday life?" (I would call this part of a building's narratability.) Certainly guidebooks and docents think so, as do art historians generally. Style really counts. But the PSFS underwent several remodelings and "re-purposings," and it more than survived artistically. Something deeper is going on, and Leatherbarrow takes us there forthwith. With Beaux-Arts genes in its form, Modernist blood in its frame, and the ideal of practical luxury, or luxurious practicality, in its mission, the building achieves a "laconic precision," a "muted splendor" that recalls less a Western than an "Oriental" ideal: dark, polished, comfortable, ready to receive elegant inhabitation of *many* kinds. If this is Mies van der Rohe, it is early Mies van der Rohe, through Lescaze. Although innovative in its use of ground-floor space and its connection to the rail line beneath, in its use of air-conditioning (it was the second building in the United States to be fully air-conditioned) and escalators, and in its use of unique corner and glazing treatments, the PSFS building certainly made urbanistic contributions to the street and to the city. But it became canonical, I suggest, for its singular and yet not idiosyncratic *beauty*—beauty of a kind architects could "do" today if they cared to. There are not many otherwise-everyday buildings of which that can be said.

Howe and Lescaze's partnership was short-lived, and, in the eyes of history, the PSFS building is the best work each was to do. In a similar way, the Art and Architecture Building at Yale would come to be seen as Paul Rudolph's best work, certainly his most iconic *and* canonic work. (I say "canonic" since Rudolph's tectonic ideas were massively copied for decades.) As Timothy Rohan tells us, in 1960 "Rudolph was at the top of his game." In the A + A building, "Rudolph seemed to have provided an alternative to the gray, soulless world of the corporatized International Style—to have devised a Modernism simultaneously colorful, textured, rough, elegant, exciting, witty, slightly vulgar, and even dangerous."

Here was a building that was to become a whipping boy for Postmodernism stylistically, and as though to prove the relevance of this judgment, it was soon overcrowded and dysfunctional. Haphazardly partitioned, and with people afraid to touch its hammered concrete walls, an interior shantytown developed that was destroyed by fire, scarring the building and closing it down.[8] Both the building and Rudolph's reputation sank fast.

It was not until the renovations of 2000 to 2004 were complete that the space Rudolph intended was seen once again. And by then, Postmodernism disgraced, the tides of architectural opinion had turned. The Art School had moved out. From the *icon* that the A + A Building always was—first in glory, then in ruin, and then in begrudged repair—it returned as *canonic*. Its Piranesian sectional development will always have something to teach; so too will its materiality and color, its sensuousness, its restrained heroism. Rohan conveys this well. "We need caves, not just goldfish bowls," he quotes Rudolph as saying, in an obvious swipe at the Lever House and its progeny. *Im*pure Modernism for impure—that is, real—people. In Rudolph we find Kahn's monumentality and Wright's intimacy combined. We hear birds twittering as water falls to the ferned pool at the bottom of a canyon. We look out through clefts and bones. We look in to protected candlelight. Is the value of a building determined forever? In some cases, it seems not.

In "Canons in Cross Fire," Charles Jencks launches us into the thick of Modern architecture's ideational complexity. Architecture's "styles" and movements are no trivial matter, he argues, but are a manifestation of a healthy and heterodox process of speciation. There *is* no Modern canon, says Jencks; there *is* no central best model, except in the minds of that species' acolytes. Purism may be the talk, but pluralism is the walk.

The resemblance to church politics is not accidental: "Direct contradictions," writes Jencks (and here he is referring to Modernism's double face: avant-garde and establishment), "are no harder for the High Church of Modernism than they are for the Vatican. In fact, both thrive on them." The truth is that protean Modern architects from Le Corbusier to Koolhaas have had to reinvent themselves every ten years or so just to stay relevant. Not only is there an element of the demonic in human creativity, writes Jencks, but the "continual revolution" so dear to Modernism, "the constant change of fashion, business cycles, technical innovations, and social transformations" that roiled the twentieth century, also "has meant that architecture, like most production in the other arts, has lacked the depth and perfection possible in earlier centuries." Quite a claim, and I think an accurate one with very few exceptions.

Jencks maps the history of Modernism as though it were the surface of a windblown sea ("It is hard to master an art while surfing the waves of 'what's next.'") and comes to rest as though he had found *his* boat, his hero, his "architect of the century" in Antonio Gaudí. Some would say that Gaudí produced only iconic architecture, but Jencks sees Gaudí as canonic. Conflating, perhaps, the man with the work, Jencks writes, "No other architect [of the time] managed to get craftsmen, artists, and even patrons working together on such a large and complete scale. His works remain the standard for the integration of all the arts at the highest creative and symbolic level."

No other architect? With Brunelleschi in the distant background, it seems clear who Gaudí's successor is: the redoubtable Frank Gehry, whose forms are not that dissimilar from Gaudí's if we zoom in a bit, and whose legacy will have little to do with his iconic style and more to do with his canonical style of practice: integrative of all the building arts, embracing of construction, advanced in all the design tools available—a medieval model, one might say, of the architect as form giver, inventor, artist, building master, and craft and construction director. Jencks does not draw this conclusion. That he does not might have to do with his preference for complex religio-symbolic form over complex rather meaning-empty form, that is, with the iconicity of it all. But I would ask: if Gaudí is going to be canonic, does that mean that works of architecture should be valued by the mastery they show of the art and process of *building*? Or is it archit*ects* who should be so evaluated? When it comes to buildings, anyway, whatever happened to the virtue of livability?

Case in point: the prolific early twentieth-century architect Henry Hornbostel. As Daniel Willis nicely lays out in "In the Shadow of a Giant: On the Consequences of Canonization," Hornbostel labored in the shadow of his much showier senior and mentor H. H. Richardson, and nowhere more obviously than in Pittsburgh. Willis compares Richardson's Allegheny County Courthouse and Jail and Hornbostel's City-County Building there with sympathy to both. But Hornbostel's grasp of what we today call "the diagram" and was then called "the *partis*" (these are not quite the same, of course, but close enough) was superior to Richardson's, who excelled at expression, at dramatics. The City-County Building, writes Willis, is "unmatched in its gracious accommodation of its citizenry. . . . Eclipsed by the greatness of its neighbors and cloaked in an air of ordinariness of its architect's own devising, [it] remains unnoticed and unappreciated."

It would seem that canonicity depends on iconicity and not the other way round. "Hornbostel's buildings," Willis goes on, "whatever they may look like, are all extraordinarily agreeable, kindly, indulgent. Such 'immeasurable' qualities are . . . generally excluded from the language of architectural criticism and praise. They are also among the most difficult architectural attributes to replicate, and this, more than any other factor, has limited Hornbostel's influence on later generations of architects."

The situation today is hardly different. Iconicity is a precondition for canonicity: if it doesn't look amazing, it's not going to be instructive, whatever its other qualities. Maybe that's why young architects labor so hard to get to first base. If architecture can be said to evolve, then it is clear that the selection process employed is sexual rather than environmental: the peahen is interested in the peacock's feathers and how he sports them, not in the peacock's intelligence or other inner qualities (of which, for better or worse, the glory of his feathers is taken to be an indicator, a sign). And thus are more little peacocks hatched that will sport beautiful tail feathers, and more peahens that will swoon for them, no matter how handicapped their suitors are by their plumage. Being immune to outside evaluation and limited in individual educability, the only other option for peacocks is gradual extinction.[9] I shall leave the reader to connect the parable to architecture.

Like biological life-forms, cultural life-forms thrive (or do not) in an environment that picks and chooses among the variations. For an environment to be an *environment,* however, there must be something oceanic or atmospheric about it, something "all-around," so that multiple forces and multiple encounters can randomly impinge upon every instance of that life-form in a hard-to-predict (e.g., close to random) way. Isolation leads to stagnation. Predictability leads to all-too-successful tricks that cannot survive change. So what becomes of an instance of the life-form "architecture" that happens to be an eyesore to some and a thing of beauty to others? More pointedly (since the pattern is the same), what happens to a work of public folk art that is at once unique, crazy, enlivening, and embarrassing?

It depends what you mean by "the public realm" and whether and how that constitutes a selecting environment. With Tyree Guyton's

1988 sculpture on Heidelberg Street in Detroit as the example (four derelict houses covered with junk and bits of paint), John Beardsley launches into the problem. In "Eyesore or Art?" we learn that then-mayor Coleman Young ordered the project's demolition. Making "no effort to hide his disdain, [and] exacerbating race and class divisions," Beardsley reports, Young suggested that "if suburbanites like the project so much, they should move it to their communities." The project was demolished, and rebuilt by an indefatigable Guyten. The current mayor is more interested in reconciliation. But he is still ambivalent: "'The City of Detroit realizes that the Heidelberg Project has artistic value . . . but it's trying to be sensitive to the concerns of citizens who live in the area.'"

Beardsley's social history of the project is both illuminating and entertaining. I cannot do it justice here. Rather, let me suggest that we have something to learn from the obvious: unlike most works of art, works of public art, and *every* work of architecture unless it is a mile from the highway, is in the public realm, even when it is funded by private institutions, used by private clients, and built on private land. Every building exists *wherever it can be seen,* wherever it casts its shadow, makes a noise, or gives an echo. In real space, "public" versus "private" is not a watertight distinction. Buildings overflow their sites. Switching metaphors: Buildings radiate their presence across and up the streets, over trees and rooftops, like blocks of pure light. Buildings can be gifts to passersby or punishments. Architects might ignore public critique for reasons I have discussed, but they cannot withdraw from exposure to it.[10] Artists can. Indeed, what are *museums* but places to protect art from the public and the public from art, making their encounter entirely voluntary, preapproved, and prearranged? This framing is not possible for architecture. To my mind, following through on the fact of architecture's radical publicness would require major supplementation of present-day architectural theory. We need a "field theory" of architecture if you will, one suited to our cell-phoned, Internetted, experience-economized age, a theory as fully cognizant of property law as it is of the geometry of perception and the oceanic nature of information.

Works of architecture have few more eloquent spokesmen for their sensuous material reality than Juhani Pallasmaa. In his contribution to this volume, "Toward an Architecture of Humility: On the Value of Experience," Pallasmaa asks us to see architecture as a thoroughly conservative art/profession at root, having the means and the mission to conserve—save—the world we think of as real and authentic against dissolving forces of the virtual, the mediated, the motivated, the marketed, the new, and the ephemeral. There is no advocacy in his position of a return to mud huts or log cabins. But there is the idea that the quality of community and sensuous experience attained living, say, in a circle of mud huts under a big sky, can be recalled—or rather, evoked or reinstated—in a perfectly Modern manner. One looks for resonance rather than reference. The archaic *can* mingle with the present and the future, as long as the standard is authenticity.

I am signatory to the mission, and so are others.[11] But Pallasmaa's piece makes me painfully aware of the possible narrowness of the vision. Spending time with Charles W. Moore in the early 1990s was, for me, the antidote. What we say accurately about human beings—that "it takes all types to make the world"—should apply to buildings too, Moore thought, and, of course, to architects. Beauty, he said, cannot be "lunged for"; it arrives as by grace. Now spread all the standard building types along a spectrum that has "permanently lived in" buildings at one end, and "visited once in a lifetime" buildings (albeit by many different people) at the other, and one sees immediately that shock value, amazingness, iconicity—call it what you will—is simply the wrong choice for houses unless the client-owner is OK with being gawked at by architecture students and tourists, does not live there much, or plans to sell soon. Ditto with places of work. Familiarity breeds boredom if not contempt, especially when the building performs the same tricks day in, day out. Do the janitors and guards at Bilbao not stifle a yawn as visitors stagger by, faces uplifted? Some buildings are vessels of time, others flashes of light, and that is the way it should be.

Then, too, consider the headline: "SUN RISES. MILLIONS GO TO WORK." You will not see this on any page of a newspaper (although one could think of some chilling scenarios in which one might). So why decry, as Pallasmaa and others do, the publicity that attends the opening of new and striking buildings and the inattention we give to everyday ones, which are surely the ones that matter more? One arrives again at the reasons that architecture is a *profession* and not a business or hobby: architects *have* to take care of the unglamorous stuff, without tire, in detail, with the best knowledge available, for everyone's sake.

After a rather abstract appreciation of Aalto, Pikionis, and Scarpa,

Pallasmaa, alas, gives me further pause (and remember, I'm a fan, a coreligionist). He concludes by listing the virtues of the architecture we should want. This listing shows—as though it needed showing—that even the most pan-human view of the values of architecture can contain unwitting cultural biases. "Our age," he writes, "seems to have lost the virtue of architectural neutrality, restraint, and modesty. Many contemporary architectural projects seem impudent and arrogant. Authentic works of art, however, remain suspended between certainty and uncertainty, faith and doubt," and goes on in a similar vein. Now, it is common to ascribe the virtues that belong to *people* to buildings (a mode of evaluation, most would agree, that loses its usefulness when the critical going gets tough).[12] Is it impudent of me, then, to observe how Scandinavian, even Finnish, are the virtues singled out by Pallasmaa? I'm not saying they're *not* virtues. I'm just saying.

It makes me wonder if my own writing is not guilty of the same bias, albeit with different virtues. Indeed, why not just say, "Some buildings are more *interesting* than others" and be done with it? This is just what Kurt Forster sets out to do in "Why Are Some Buildings More Interesting Than Others?" But because he puts the proposition in the interrogative, he cannot be done with it, and we read on. Forster's essay is about evaluation itself as it is practiced by historians/critics of architecture. Might it be that, to this group at least, the first and last sin in architecture is *being uninteresting*?

Let us say yes. The problem, of course, as Forster points out, is that how interesting X is depends less on X than on how X is conceptually framed, culturally contextualized, scientifically and historically researched, and presented by some*one* . . . which is to say, on how interesting the historian/critic is. Let's face it, some people can make *anything* interesting (which is why good essayists are as rare as their potential subjects are legion), and other people can make everything boring. What are the stratagems of the former type even as they risk becoming the latter?[13]

In architecture there are several. Among them are providing historical background, preferably in vivid narrative form; weaving a web of ideas, metaphors, and analogies in which to locate the subject; contrasting different scales and levels of perception (macro, micro, personal, public); confounding personal virtues with architectural virtues, as we have just discussed; and then this one: detecting "logical" paradoxes, contradictions, and "tensions" in the work (or the things said about it) *and then leaving them deliciously, scintillatingly in place*. In this way a person of medium build becomes "tall, yet short; both, yet neither."

The last is a popular stratagem still, in these twilight years of poststructuralism, and Forster makes good use of it. But Forster also constructs a sly picture of the present moment in architecture, when *references* to things by buildings, as "picked up on" and explicated by critics, increasingly fail to satisfy. In the work of Peter Eisenman, for example, he sees the weakness as clear: complex figurations, formal moves, and pseudo-evolutionary design procedures based on the diagramming of invisible processes in other realms (e.g., molecular biology) yielding up buildings that are only incidentally livable and only strainedly meaningful. Herzog and de Meuron's Signal Box building in Basel goes the next step: into enigma without apology. "[Its] impenetrable quality rewrites the equation of all its functions, invisible and symbolic," Forster writes, "and yet preserves a fundamental impenetrability for the traveler's passing glance. The Signal Box assumes the silent presence of a sanctuary in the desecrated terms of our time: what we have harnessed continues to escape our grasp. . . . the Signal Box codifies the powers it seeks to abolish by housing them in an inviolable shroud." Tall yet short, anyone?

In the end, architecture without *imagination*—the imagination of the architect, and, I think Forster wants to add, the imagination of critics and historians like himself—is simply not interesting enough to *deserve* evaluation. Why? Because "only acts of *imaginative transmission*" (Forster's emphasis) "allow us to figure out how we came to fall into the place we occupy and what prospects lie before us." How serious is *that*? I am reminded of Oscar Wilde's semi-jest, spoken by Vivian in *The Decay of Lying*: "Things are because we see them, and what we see, and how we see it, depends on the Arts that have influenced us. . . . Truth is entirely and absolutely a matter of style, while Life—poor, probable, uninteresting human life . . . will (always) follow meekly after."[14]

As though to touch ground again, the editor of this volume next features the ideas of historian and architect Kenneth Frampton. Technically minded, socially minded, experienced at the drawing board, suspicious of art-world cant, prolific as a writer, and globally well traveled, Frampton, in an interview by William Saunders and Nancy Levinson ("Questions of Value"), sparkles with wisdom. Canons depend on traditions, Frampton notes, and both canons and traditions evolve. Iconic works by iconic architects are not the proper locus of critical attention, at least not *all* of it, as is currently the case. The condition of architecture as a whole, and the conditions of architectural *practice,* which differ from country to country, he argues, are eminently worthwhile studying in their own right. Politics, economics, institutional development, technological availabilities, and labor play roles as least as large as that of pure architectural creativity in determining what gets built and how. In particular, in America, the framework for construction provided by a free-market economy means that people do *not* get what they really want or really need, but what they are persuaded to want by advertising, can afford to want, can finance or otherwise finagle to save or make a buck. Too many in the profession have become mere providers, and too many of architecture's clients have become consumers, or the agents of, or the renters to consumers. It would not be wrong to see in all this a socialist's commitment, antipathy to frippery, to the Wildean worldview. Of the "subversive" avant-garde designers of the day Frampton says (and it helps to remember that he teaches at Columbia): "Neo-avant-garde work . . . favors spectacular aestheticism . . . graphic in its formation . . . rather than architecture as such. . . . Given its post-Duchampian heuristics and its evocation of chaos theory, etc., this aesthetic speculation is rendered all the more intangible by vague divagations upon the relativity of value in the late-modern world. Such neo-avant-gardism has indubitably yielded an architecture that pertains to the schizophrenic sensibility of our epoch; however, I am doubtful that either education or any form of critique, let alone socially responsible modes of practice, can be predicated on a cultural discourse that is, in the last analysis, so indulgently elusive."

Economic realities weigh in everywhere, Frampton argues, and ought not simply to be accepted. Even the giddy pursuit of formalism will find itself hemmed in on all sides—computers notwithstanding—unless the profession first understands and then adjusts its mode of production. Perhaps buildings *should* cost more. Who is there to make *that* case? And on what basis could such a case be made if not (if I might chime in) by (1) articulating the subtle and life-enhancing things good buildings—really good buildings—actually *do,* and how they do them, and (2) conveying a sample of that expertise to architecture's clients and public, not to mention architects? Would this not make buildings interesting enough? Of course it would. But it might leave many practitioners of present-day architectural criticism high and dry, and it might necessitate other sorts of scholarship, journalism, and award giving. One must look long and hard, Frampton suggests, at such projects as the University of Aviero by Álvaro Siza. But who has the time?

Frampton concedes that it would contravene human nature to be uninterested in the new. But there is something about the whole package of architecture that needs our critical/evaluative attention now, something that is not its newness or promise in far-out form. How ironic it is, then, that never in history have so many creative and clever people like architects had so little time to research, read, absorb, or reflect upon things that matter—that they *know* matter—before plowing on. Call it information war; call it information sickness: productivity beating receptivity in every sphere; working at work, working at home, working on the road, working on "vacation," time more scarce than money, the accumulation of thought an impossibility. Was that your cell phone?

Sorry, mine. Where was I? Is there something about the whole subject of values and valuation that suits the temperament of conservatives (and I don't mean Republicans)? Are values always "old things"? And is discussing them rationally, even cleverly, ever more than a cover for lamentation over the passing of one's favorite ones?

To read the British philosopher of aesthetics Roger Scruton ("Most Architecture Should Be Modest"), one would suspect so. More indignantly than Frampton and Pallasmaa, Scruton takes dead aim at the capitalist paradigm (i.e., Americans): "Subtract the profit makers and the vandals" (notice the pairing) "and ask ordinary people how their town should be designed" (ordinary people know best of course), "and a surprising level of agreement will be reached." To wit: nothing too big or small, too broad or tall, something discreet in its lighting, "human" in its materials, something classical . . . something *nice*. The common good is not just common *and* good, but gooder than any good sui generis. Scruton comes away from Heidegger's statement that "we attain to dwelling . . . only by means of building" with the conclusion that people who hire architects are bound to do something "intrusive" to the good people who don't.[15] But what distinction could be more crucial for architecture as a *profession* than that between private and public goods? And who is more strongly pledged than architects to devise a reconciliation between public and private goods in a way that, as times change, requires creativity? (Of course, I mean good architects, professional ones, not mere service providers or developers' lackeys.)[16]

Scruton presents the reactionary-conservative position succinctly. There is much in what he says that ought to be challenging to progressives and avant-gardists. With the passing of neoclassical architecture and its replacement by the Modernist idiom, it is true that whole "species" of life-enhancing space types, material palettes, and dwelling morphologies have become nearly extinct the world over. Having abandoned the built-in wisdom of such long-evolved models, says Scruton, what remains of the once great art of Architecture is not much more than a money-driven free-for-all, "a practice dominated by talentless people" who imagine themselves auteurs.

The picture Scruton paints is bleak. Call it late Ruskinian. But unlike, say, Christopher Alexander or Robert Venturi, Scruton offers no way forward except perhaps Prince Charles's. Standards of aesthetic judgment may well be objective and timeless as Scruton warrants, and he claims to know them, but it seems to me that the virtues of the vernacular classicism he favors—and they are real—need to be limned in categories quite foreign to both philosophy of aesthetics and art history if they are to be reborn in a new architectonic body, under a new technological regime.

In "From Taste to Judgment: Multiple Criteria in the Evaluation of Architecture," William Saunders makes an equally impassioned—and dare I now say characteristically American—case for the diversity of values that apply to architecture, as a profession, as a product, as an art, as a business, as an academic discipline . . . simultaneously. How to manage such complexity? What critical sensibilities are best attuned to what problems facing architecture? How can anyone make value *decisions* with respect to architecture—and let us remember that *decide* comes from *de cidere,* "to cut off"—without cutting off the option to make decisions that might be different in the future, and do *that* without sliding down the slippery slope of value relativism now?

Like the experienced editor he is, Saunders turns to the better-known critics of this time and constructs a taxonomy of three basic critical positions. To these he attaches names. *Subjectivism:* Ada Louise Huxtable and Herbert Muschamp. Here, the critic claims a nature especially sensitive to architecture, and the critic's emotional intuitive response to a building dominates. Shortness of analysis, hyperbole in praise, and vagueness in ascription of causes are constant temptations. *Politics and morality:* Mike Davis, Diane Ghirardo, Kenneth Frampton. Here the critic's conscience dominates; buildings are social acts involving power and exclusion. Dogmatism is the danger of this position, blindness to pleasure, and vagueness (again), but now about how buildings *actually* have moral consequence.[17] *Pluralism without relativism:* Michael Sorkin. If sensitivity marks the first position, and sobriety the second, then romanticism, or "affirmation," marks the third: a belief in human possibility, an interest in everything. Saunders leaves for last his favorite critical position. He quotes Sorkin: "'Art, after all, is our great hedge against the oppressions of a universal sure thing'" and adds, "Sensitivity to the dangers of 'a universal sure thing' is, I believe, a key trait of good criticism." Good critics should be as aware of their own proclivities as they are of their subject's, bring them forth, and put them down on the page. Living is all, and more life—or "maximum aliveness," as Saunders calls it—is the chief if not only goal worth striving for.

Precisely. But there are dangers and temptations in the pluralist position too. At the meta-level (i.e., at the level of criticism of critics), one must note that when broadmindedness is the virtue heralded, profligacy is the only rebuke that sticks, and the one who offers it is likely to be framed as a killjoy; while at the first level (i.e., that of actual observations about buildings), the romantic view leads one powerfully to the "pathetic fallacy" once again,[18] in this case, reading qualities of the architect into the buildings they designed and vice versa. Thus are Aalto's *buildings,* according to Sorkin and quoted by Saunders, "'supple, human, careful . . . friendly . . . gracious, never authoritarian.'" (Those Finns!) Recovering somewhat, Saunders concludes with a rallying cry to his peers, tuned to a perfect pitch: "If architecture that achieves artistic, affective, inspirational power while satisfying functional needs is that architecture that most embodies fullness and richness of life, then criticism will attend to and celebrate that architecture above all."

May it be so.

The volume closes with two essays that circle back to its opening themes, on the editorial hope, perhaps, that the reader has grown wiser.

"Once Again by the Pacific: Returning to Sea Ranch" by Tim Culvahouse and Lisa Findley tells the story of the rise and fall from the critical landscape—less fall, really, than fading—of Moore Lyndon Turnbull Whitaker's (MLTW's) landmark condominiums on the coast of northern California. Here was a group of buildings that achieved iconicity and canonicity for decades, not to mention career-cementing accolades for its chief architect, Charles Moore. Why did Sea Ranch slowly disappear from view? Culvahouse and Findley suggest that it might have been how Moore's practice developed—"the provocative—some would say kitschy—buildings that Charles Moore designed after he left MLTW: the Piazza d'Italia, the Wonderwall for the New Orleans World's Fair, and so on." The work of Lyndon and Turnbull became too unassuming, they say, while Whitaker turned to teaching. Does the failure of an iconic work to become canonical in its architect's *own* oeuvre eventually undermine its claim to canonicity in general? This seems not quite right: Wright and Le Corbusier had Picasso-like "periods," as have Graves and Gehry. As Jencks pointed out, great architects reinvent themselves. Most. I suppose it is a matter of risk. Moore tasted architectural liberty in imagination, in fairy tale, in lightness of being—elements all present at Sea Ranch, bubbling under the Puritan material honesty of the barn as a type and giving it new poise, new life—and, as they say, "ran with it" . . . right past where most architects wanted to go. This is one explanation. Another is the parallel process in the world of architectural theory and criticism, where, as Culvahouse and Findley sketch out, the tides of pop and then historical Postmodernism rose and then fell and then rose again, only to be dashed on the pilings of deconstructivism and then soothed (finally?) into glassy-smooth certitude of today: the Modern is here to stay (but throw in a few compound curves).

As against the vagaries of this story, Culvahouse and Findley re-experience Sea Ranch firsthand and up close, providing us with a vivid account of the life-oriented thinking it embodies. With only occasional use of "yet" and "deploy" (those two emblems of Ivy League Theory) and with a minimum of human virtue listing, the authors explore the typology, influences, and landscape of Sea Ranch in a tour de force of professional architectural appreciation: observant, plainspoken, technical, experiential, historical, and generous—a canonical elegy, one might say, for a deservedly canonical work.

Diane Ghirardo, whom William Saunders in this volume groups with critics committed to the political/moral stance, gets the final word. In "The Absence of Presence: The Knickerbocker Residence and the Fate of Nonelitist Architecture," we are treated to a fine example of how the approach works.

"The Knickerbocker Residence?" you ask. Precisely, says Ghirardo:

you don't know it. It is an SRO (single-room-occupancy) forty-eight-unit apartment building for otherwise homeless and/or mentally ill veterans in Brooklyn, New York, designed by Jonathan Kirschenfeld (who?) of Architrope (what?) and built for $117/square foot in 1994–95. Each apartment is better than it has to be in every way, says Ghirardo, from its architect-designed fixtures to its slightly taller-than-standard ceilings. "Although small, the units radiate warmth and light." Moreover, the complex operates largely within the language of the surrounding buildings and was achieved by applying enormous ingenuity both in design and in negotiating the regulations that apply to such buildings.

Diligent in seeking the approval of his peers, and not without Ivy League educations, friends in high places, and prize-winning track records of their own, Kirschenfeld and his partner, Andrew Bartle, submitted the Knickerbocker project to architecture magazines. Receiving brief mention for moral worthiness, no more, they sought the ears of Paul Goldberger and Herbert Muschamp. Neither would bite. Both were too busy reporting on the stars or sharing a dais with them. Focusing on the opening, at roughly the same time, of Peter Eisenman's Aronoff Center for Design and Art at the University of Cincinnati (which building I can here merely assert, having spent time in it, is one of the worst ever designed for its purpose), Ghirardo proceeds to skewer the vacuity and condescension of the speakers ("Peter's friends") not just with distaste but marvel: "What *is* remarkable . . . is that such groups have been able to convince so many of their cultural superiority."

The reception of Knickerbocker Residence is for Ghirardo symptomatic of old-fashioned class warfare: that dense and useless game of prestige management played in cities like New York among the culturati in general, not just name architects. The Knickerbocker Residence is simply "about" the wrong *people* within the wrong taste culture. "To the world of architecture as currently constituted," she writes, "such client groups and their invariably downscale districts are not worth lionizing in order to cultivate them for future work. . . . At its core, architecture today is supremely elitist."

"Well, yes," one wants to reply, "and it long has been." Which is no excuse, of course: slavery was around for a long time too. And yet, and yet . . . I cannot help thinking that Ghirardo's anger overwhelms the facts and the fact that the times *are* changing. At around the same time that Architrope was finishing its project, several SRO hotels designed by Rob Wellington Quigley in San Diego were receiving warm publishing attention, complete with photographs and design feature analysis. Michael Pyatok, then as now, was neither unknown nor poor, and both Quigley and Pyatok's design awards require much scrolling on their Web pages. Samuel Mockbee has ascended to architectural sainthood, and a large and growing constituency around the country is trying to emulate the Rural Studio where *they* are. The *New York Times* did a magazine feature on the Studio, and coffee-table books still arrive. *Nest* had a good run; *Dwell* is thriving; pilgrimages to Marfa continue. These are encouraging signs. Among the next generation of architects I detect a burgeoning interest in architecture that is good—good in a moral sense, with the conviction that this architecture will have a beauty as unmistakable as a lily's precisely for not being "lunged for," that it will hold our interest precisely for being genuinely, complexly, humanly, phenomenologically interesting in itself, not razored to within an inch of its habitational life. A Pritzker Prize might not be just around the corner for this kind of architecture. But it will come.

Judging Architectural Value is the title of this book. Can architectural value be judged fairly, judged objectively? I think this book shows that it can—as long as one leaves the proposition somewhat vague and in the passive voice, and as long as one does not imagine "judged" to mean fixed forever. Flux is the norm. All values evolve except the value of life itself. Which brings us to a final thought:

The gains offered to life by evolution are less ratchetlike than wavy, less assured than statistical. What promotes "maximum aliveness" here and now may not promote "maximum aliveness" there or forever. We might take comfort, though, from knowing that we always have this deepest of life principles to turn to, to study, and to apply. Just how many ways are there for buildings to help preserve, honor, and promote all forms and instances of life except those that destroy others (for this is how "aliveness" is maximized)? I don't know. The counting of the ways has just begun.

Notes

1. When a design *competition* is the means of commissioning, and the jury is representative of different classes, cultures, or areas of expertise, a clash of values is all but a forgone conclusion. Which is why so few competitions result in the best architect doing the best job.

2. An answer to the question "who cares?" will emerge from the rest of our discussion.

3. Businesspeople and tradesmen also ask for our trust, of course, but only to the extent of the law. Here a reputation for honesty, as well as a competitive quality/price ratio for the goods or services delivered, is sufficient. Codes of ethics, Better Business Bureau memberships, and the like are optional: good if they increase business, otherwise not. Businesses advertise and cajole, but professionals are only recommended. Professionals *profess* (from the Latin "declare publicly") that they have extensive knowledge of something difficult, that they deserve our trust, that they will act/advise/serve for the good of all and not themselves alone . . . hang out their shingle, and wait.

4. This covers obeying all the laws that obtain and being honest in all their professional dealings.

5. Some popular newspaper-based critics have larger ambitions than speaking for architects to the people and for people to the architects. They wish to become "players" themselves in the development or art-cultural scene.

6. Perhaps some future publication will give voice to the second.

7. Interestingly, since there is no professional association of architecture writers, my professionalism in this regard is subsumed under that of university professors', whose primary responsibility "is to seek and to state the truth as they see it," and to support the free exchange of ideas. (See www.iit.edu/departments/csep/codes/coe/aaup-g.html.)

8. The fire was accidental, although lore has it as deliberate—an expression of the campus rebellions of the 1960s.

9. For an accessible exploration of the mechanisms and consequences of sexual selection, from plants to humans, see Geoffrey Miller, *The Mating Mind* (New York: Anchor Books, 2001).

10. The same is true of our *appearance* (a lovely term), since it happens to others. We ought not to allow ourselves to dress and groom how *we* please, at least not when *in public* (another lovely phrase, hinting of immersion).

11. Michael Benedikt, *For an Architecture of Reality* (New York: Lumen Books, 1987); Peter Zumthor, *Thinking Architecture* (Basel: Lars Muller Publisher, 1998).

12. The attribution of human qualities to inanimate things was memorably called "the pathetic fallacy" by John Ruskin. For more about the class dimension of the pathetic fallacy in architecture, see my "Class Notes" in *Harvard Design Magazine* 11 (Summer 2000): 4–9.

13. Interestingly, each type gambles with its class status. For when "interesting" is the overarching value, the person wielding the judgment is presumed to be above concern with more basic, utilitarian values, and even aesthetic ones. Topping that, class-wise, is to find the world *boring*—if, that

is, you also have means and power. There is nothing quite so tiresome, dear, as *enthusiasm,* nor so bourgeois as *knowing* things. I would not bring this up were architectural (and art world) criticism not so riddled with class-specific value systems.

14. Quoted by Joshua Glen, "Oscar Wilde (1854–1900)," www.hermenaut .com/a163.shtml.

15. Look twice at the word *we* when it comes from a philosopher, and three times if the philosopher is Heidegger. Heidegger's claim is quite wrong too, in that the vast majority of people do not dwell in anything *they* built at all. The phenomenology of the real construction process remains to be done, as does a study of the difference between owning and renting, making and finding, designing and fabricating.

16. Nor is dwelling only "collective," as Scruton passingly asserts. It is also—indeed I would say mostly—intensely private and personal. See Gaston Bachelard's *The Poetics of Space.*

17. The reader can see my own view at work: I just don't think architects (or critics) *know enough* about what buildings actually do or how they do it. Theory in architecture knows as much about the phenomenon *building* as Galen knew about the body.

18. See note 12. When critics discuss critics, or when critics (or historians) evaluate archi*tects,* as people, as creators, etc., a degree of ad hominen argument is appropriate. The question is: do *buildings* affect people just as people do, or as their architects do? Can an annoying architect make a serene building? I think so. The distinction between art and artist is a crucial one to all literary and art criticism, of course. It is an oft-crossed boundary, however, and not always detected.

1

Learning from St. Louis: The Arch, the Canon, and Bourdieu

Hélène Lipstadt

> All I can wish for is that iconoclastic critique, which can use the weapons of sociological analysis, will be able to promote an artistic experience shorn of ritualism and exhibitionism.
> —Pierre Bourdieu, 1990

> Within the city the experience of discovering and rediscovering the Arch is varied considerably by one's location. . . . The unexpectedness of these far-and-near glimpses is the most exciting part of the viewing experience for those who live with the Arch and can savor its endless variety from day to day.
> —George McCue, 1978

One need not be an architecture critic—George McCue was not—to have an "artistic experience" of the sorcery of Eero Saarinen's Gateway Arch in St. Louis, Missouri: its ability to render itself invisible with changes in weather and light; to assume, when seen from different angles, different shapes; and to appear and disappear in the landscape. A professor at St. Louis University described how "always there is something different about" the Arch in "every picture people take." This seems to be the case whether the people are tourists, the Arteaga family of commercial photographers, who have shot the Arch for more than thirty years, or the more famous Joel Meyerowitz. Meyerowitz has "seen the Arch change from a white you could not look at to black, in broad daylight." So has Joe Mason, an "ordinary citizen," who recounted how an out-of-town friend who saw the Arch for the first time from the air was convinced that the 630-foot-high gleaming stainless-steel chameleon was indeed black, because on that "particular day, from the air, the Arch looked black."[1]

The existence of variability and perceptible ephemerality in the Jefferson National Expansion Memorial—to give the Arch its full name—challenges various art historical categories and chronologies, including some fundamental Postmodern verities. Designed in 1947–48 by a Modernist architect, the Arch throws into question art historian and theorist Rosalind Krauss's influential argument that Modernist sculpture was a "monument . . . [an] abstraction . . . functionally placeless and largely self-referential" until sculptors entered the "historical rupture" known as Postmodernism and "thought the expanded field" by combining sculpture with landscape and "not-landscape" or architecture and "not-architecture." The Arch also casts doubt on the confident assertions made by designers of Postmodern counter-monuments that it was their similarly conceived works of the 1990s that enabled viewers to see memorials as mutable and ephemeral, and not necessarily as fixed and eternal; in short, the Arch suggests that the counter-monuments were not the first to fundamentally change commemorative art.[2]

The reassessment of the Arch could thus begin and end with this description of the mutability of the monument and the phenomenology of its perception. I am, however, interested in a reassessment of broader categories—the categories of "icons" and "canons." These terms are used synonymously by historians and theorists of art to signify works that, by consensus, are thought "great." But are these words really synonyms?

The issue of canons and icons is timely. Since the 1970s, canonization in art and literature has been famously challenged by feminists, who favor the "exploding" of canons, the exposing of their exclusionary, repressive, and discriminatory nature, even the abandoning of them altogether. The canons have been equally famously defended. Scholars have shown that for the early church, the canon consisted of those writings deemed trustworthy for believers, and that the proposition that canons are inherently exclusionary confuses that meaning with the later use of the word to designate church law. Doing away with that false analogy has allowed Henry Louis Gates Jr. to conclude that

Gateway Arch, circa 1977, from Busch Stadium. Photograph by Joel Meyerowitz. Courtesy of Edwynn Hour Gallery.

a "canon" is a literary "tradition" that comes into being "because writers read other writers and ground their representations of experience in models of language provided largely by other writers to whom they feel akin."[3]

The subject of icons is less fraught and less politicized than that of canons—although today it is nonetheless preferable in the academy to be an iconoclast than an admirer of icons. The word *icon* has acquired additional definitions since the Greek term for "image, representation" was applied to ritual images that served a liturgical function in the Byzantine Church and also entered the homes of believers as objects of worship beginning in the fourth century. Today, *icon* means one category of things to semioticians, another to software designers, and a third to historians of religious icons. To most people, however, *icon* also has a commonsensical meaning that can be construed from the persons or things to which the term is applied, whether Jacqueline Kennedy Onassis, the Statue of Liberty, or the Nike swoosh. Icons of this sort are icons of popular culture and, by definition, need no introduction, explanation, or commentary. The textless Nike advertisement made that point. Icons of place—

the Eiffel Tower, for example—exemplify such meaning-taken-for-granted icons. Certain icons of popular culture are especially revered; Michael Jordan comes to mind. But however much they may be "worshipped," such popular icons part company from religious icons in one significant way. The latter were and are prayed to because they are a manifestation of a divine prototype, of an archetype that exists in a separate, inaccessible *spiritual* realm that the icon brings to earth. Michael Jordan and swooshes are icons because a community has agreed to a certain reading, according to which the image or person is more realistic than all others and therefore more *earthly* than others. Nonetheless, orthodox and popular icons share one thing that canons do not possess: a broad community of consensual believers.

Since the 1970s, canons have came under scrutiny in architecture, too. We have come a long way from the time when critic and historian Reyner Banham could declare that the "canonical list of who is, and who isn't, a member of the modern movement" established by Nikolaus Pevsner in 1936 had "not been seriously questioned, only extended a little" by himself, Pevsner's student, and by his own student Charles Jencks in books that descended from each other in "almost apostolic succession." "Pevsner's Route 66" is "today . . . reject[ed] and deride[d] . . . as the master narrative of modern architecture, a history told by the victors," *New York Times* architecture critic Herbert Muschamp recently wrote.[4]

Or so we thought. Now a spate of books and Web sites purport to identify the "great buildings" and "masterworks" that "shaped" the twentieth century—and that are equated with "icons." Shrugging off these publications as millennium-induced chronicles intended for the midcentury modern coffee tables of the readers of *Wallpaper* misses the point. If, after almost forty years of always passionate and sometimes bitter conflict over canons, we can still canonize without so much as a thought about the mechanisms and modalities of canons, then something profound and unceasing is at work.

A reconsideration of the Gateway Arch suggests what is at stake when we persist in canonizing, for the Arch has long been an icon of St. Louis and for St. Louisians. But it is, to use words that echoed through the McCarthy era when it was designed, "not now, nor has it ever been, a member" of the canon. Understanding the *Arch as an icon that is not canonic* initiates a special sort of historicization rich in emancipatory potential.

Employing the sociology of Pierre Bourdieu as my theoretical framework and the Arch as my example allows me to suggest not only that canonic and iconic works are not synonymous, but also that they are not accorded equal value. Although canons are indeed inescapable and even necessary for architecture (or any discipline), they go hand in hand with a disregard for iconic works. Further, the categories of "icon" and "canon" smuggle into architecture a discriminating mode of evaluating things that is actually a discriminatory mode of evaluating people. The icon/canon relationship merits a hard critical look.

I believe that canons and icons are examples of what Bourdieu calls "the unconscious presuppositions that the history [of works of art and culture] is able to impose." A historicization of the discipline of architecture's admiration of canonical works and of our concomitant lack of regard for buildings that are popular icons is the kind of "social history" of the apprehension of artworks that Bourdieu hopes his sociology will incite (and has incited in France). Far from teaching social fatalism, as many believe he has done, Bourdieu counsels his students to undertake a liberatory historicization, one that "rids" those who apprehend (or to use his word, "read") works of art of "historically imposed" categories. This explicitly "social" history of artworks provides those readers with "defensive instruments against the effects of clandestine persuasion . . . and strategies of manipulation" within works themselves.[5] Since architects are "readers" who go on to author works, they could be double beneficiaries of such a historicization. Made aware of the manipulation to which they are subjected, they could acquire an important element of the knowledge needed to cease perpetuating that manipulation themselves. In Bourdieu's terms, they would be able to move toward his goal of self-emancipation from domination through self-reflexivity.

The canon/icon distinction, as well as the attitudes toward buildings and those who "read" them embedded in that differentiation, can lead to the manipulation of evaluation, because both are instances of the classifications that create what Bourdieu calls "distinction." Here we have yet another case in which the seemingly "pure" categories of aesthetic evaluation, which we believe to express "taste," serve to maintain and perpetuate social difference in symbolic ways all the more powerful and pernicious for being subtle, for exerting, in Bourdieu's terms, "symbolic power."

To understand how the Arch, a work by a renowned architect,

failed to become canonic and yet became iconic, one must look back to the decades when there was a single, all-powerful, and incontrovertible definition of Modern architecture. Texas architect and educator Paul Kennon recollects: "You were either in the Mies . . . Wright . . . or . . . Corbu camp and . . . your vocabulary as an architect was limited within the principles of those three." The Mies camp was dominant, according to Kevin Roche. "Mies's [was] accepted as the ultimate solution [to] . . . realizing the golden age, and there did not seem to be any reason to do anything different." Robert Venturi would later say that "less was a bore." In fact, Miesian orthodoxy was a form of thought control; thinking outside of the Miesian box was difficult, thinking beyond the International Style, seemingly impossible. "To act contrary to that [Miesian solution] and still have ambitions of being a serious architect was an extremely difficult thing to do; it was a soul-searching process," remembers Roche. Cesar Pelli recalls that "You could not be against the International Style in the 1950s. . . . [I]t would be like being against architecture."[6]

These architects knew how those who "acted contrary" fared, for they were all associates of Eero Saarinen, and no one unsettled the orthodoxy more thoroughly, more frequently, and with greater apostasy than he. His General Motors Technical Center (1946–57, with Smith, Hinchman and Grylls) was inspired by Mies's Illinois Institute of Technology. It was Miesian in plan, structure, composition, and detailing. Here Saarinen had demonstrated how the canon worked by emulating Mies even before there was an 880 Lakeshore Drive to emulate. This "major expansion of the Miesian ideals" was "exactly the concept that the hour require[d]," and General Motors therefore became an object of "unstinted and unthinking adulation." And as General Motors went, so went the nation's architects. Soon, however, Saarinen departed from the very Miesian consensus he had helped to consolidate. He began to "stun architectural opinion," to become the period's "bewilderingly varied architect," or as less polite critics said, its eclectic.[7] His betrayal of the Miesian orthodoxy was redoubled by a second, perhaps greater—if unwitting—perfidy. As Reyner Banham has argued, Saarinen's "diversity" exposed the fallacy of American Modernism's central dogma, "form follows function," by obeying that dogma to the hilt. His much-decried "styles-for-the-job" approach was, in fact, a response to or a symbolic expression of the functional particularities that exist in every program, as the two very different airport terminals, TWA at Kennedy Airport (1957–60) and Dulles International (1958–62, with Ammann and Whitney), made stunningly evident. By contrast, the endless repetitions and iterations of the International Style were revealed to have not followed function, but instead to have ignored it. No wonder, as Banham said, that Saarinen made the critics "nervous."[8] The Arch, however, did not make the critics nervous. Actually, it did not interest them at all.

The Arch began its life in the public eye: the 1947–48 competition was extensively covered by the architectural press. Subsequently, not only the architectural press but also the national newspapers reported on the controversial accusation that Saarinen's "parabolic" arch had been plagiarized from a triumphal arch designed for Mussolini's planned Esposizione Urbanistica Roma. Equal attention was paid to the architect's rebuttal that not only were the geometries of the two arches different, but also that parabolic arches were often enough used in interwar architecture to give Saarinen an abundance of designs to "plagiarize." Progress (or lack of it) was tracked by the architecture magazines from 1948 to the start of construction in 1963, the topping off in 1965, and the award of a special AIA Henry Bacon Medal for memorial architecture in 1966. But if the Arch was news, it was not architecture—that is, architecture worth talking about. The Arch is missing from the critical clamor that surrounded Saarinen during his lifetime and from the more flattering assessments that began with TWA and continued after his death in 1961. All of which makes this one exception to the silence of the 1960s significant.

In *American Architecture and Urbanism,* Vincent Scully described the Arch as a "startling sculpture of gigantic size," which, because of its "vastness, scalelessness, and uselessness, does in fact function as a potent sculptural intrusion," though one "capable of menacing everything else and dominating space from afar." The Arch reminded him of the "great grain elevators of the . . . plains . . . without referential scale, gleaming, far-seen American cathedrals, devoid of images and congregation." Although Scully extolled the "scalelessness and disorientation" that made the Arch a precursor of the parodying sculptures of Claes Oldenburg and of Robert Venturi's 1964 fountain project for Fairmont Parkway in Philadelphia, and that thus made Saarinen "ahead of his time and much in the American spirit," he deemed the Arch to have less "hallucinatory force" than these later works.[9] Scully, always the astute observer and ever the inscrutable Delphic oracle, admitted the Arch into his textbook of American architectural history, but on terms that can only be called praising with faint damn. The Arch earns its place there as a failed icon (the empty cathedral of the grain elevator), but not as an icon itself, and still less as a member of the canon.

With few exceptions—monographs on Saarinen's contemporaries and former employees, the critical overviews of midcentury architecture written in the 1960s, survey textbooks of Modern and American architecture, and, a fortiori, the proliferating compilations of "masterworks"—the Arch has been passed over in silence.[10] The Arch, then, has been and remains the object of a virtually total highbrow disregard. And even defenders of canons understand this kind of invisibility as an indicator that a work is not canonic. A word on canons is thus in order.

Canons, strictly speaking, are formed of and by texts. *Canon*, from the Greek *kanon*, meaning "cane," came into use in the third century to designate holy writings that were the source of unimpeachably orthodox teaching, texts soon understood to constitute the Bible, a body of limited, unalterable, authoritative writings. The use of *canon* to designate classical works of literature and, by extension, classical

Gateway Arch, the final section being put in place, October 1965. To install its final section, the mammoth legs of the Arch were pried open by a 450-ton hydraulic force; because of their weight (more than 8,000 tons each), the legs had deflected inward and were only 2.5 feet apart before the last 8-foot section was installed. Copyright Arteaga Photos Ltd.

works in all the arts, is relatively recent and coincides with the emergence in the eighteenth century of the concept of aesthetic value. It is therefore helpful to attend to the comments of a scholar who has commented on the canon in both of these contexts.

Canonical texts acquire a status that can take "many guises," writes Moshe Halbertal.[11] There are, according to Halbertal, four types of canons formed by texts: "normative," "formative," and two types of "exemplary" canons, "broad" and "narrower." The normative canon consists of texts that are "obeyed and followed," as exemplified by scriptures and legal codes. Formative canons are "a constitutive part of a curriculum . . . [which are] not followed in the strict sense but are taught, read, transmitted, and interpreted. They provide a society or a profession with a shared vocabulary . . . [and are] shared cultural assets. . . . Familiarity with that canon is a precondition for membership." The broadly conceived exemplary canon is composed of "paradigmatic examples of aesthetic value and achievement, models for imitation that set criteria for what is regarded as the highest form of art." The narrowly construed exemplary canon is constituted by "exemplars of schools and trends . . . [that] highlight the characteristics of the genre lucidly and forcefully, although they do not represent the best of that genre but rather what most typifies it."

Applying these distinctions to architecture today is instructive. Building codes can be said to establish one of architecture's normative canons (although their normativity is limited, since one of the challenges of design is to adhere to them inventively). Pedagogy in history and, to a lesser extent, in design is grounded in the exemplary canon. Some canonical works acquire the stature of paradigms, insofar as we draw from them the criteria of the best that architecture can be at a particular moment. Imitation follows, although strict plagiarism is discouraged. Finally, as a profession, architecture is dependent on a formative canon composed of skills, procedures, and modes of cognition that, to recall Halbertal, is not "followed in the strict sense," as is a normative canon, but certainly constitutes a "precondition for membership."

In none of Halbertal's senses is the Arch canonic. Obviously not obeyed, it is neither "studied and read" as part of the formative canon, nor, as near as we can tell from the designs of the postwar period, was it ever "imitated and revered" or looked upon as "a standard . . . [something that] bestow[s] value." We must now ask why this is the case. Why did architects and critics not feel "akin" to it? Why have historians overlooked it?

The indifference of architects seems to require little explanation. The Arch was a monument, and monuments were not what Modernists made. Moreover, its colossal size impeded out-and-out duplication. Yet neither argument is entirely persuasive, for monuments in fact have been the object of both competitions and commissions (to Erich Mendelsohn and Louis I. Kahn, for example), and nothing prevented the adaptation of individual components of the design—the unusual geometry of a weighted catenary or the innovative stainless steel skin, for example. The disregard by critics seems equally self-explanatory. The decade-long delay (1948–58) between competition and the start of actual design would constitute a serious failing for them, since being unbuilt was a definite disadvantage in the can-do postwar decades, and a delayed posthumous work neither confirms nor establishes the trends that critics must track to remain critics. Still, the circumstance of being unbuilt had not undercut the reputations of Le Corbusier's League of Nations Headquarters and Mies's Friedrichstrasse tower. As America's most prominent unbuilt design, the Arch could easily have been put to good use by the many critics who rushed to rehabilitate Saarinen's reputation after his early death in 1961. It was not.

The Arch's failure to attract the attention of architectural historians of the period, however, is entirely surprising, for all the ingredients of a traditional heroicizing art historical monograph are found in its tale: the unexpected victory by a young architect in a major competition; a soupçon of Oedipal struggle between Eero Saarinen and his father, Eliel, who both submitted competition entries, one Modern and the other traditional; and a triumphant design that synthesized Modernism's ideals of advanced technology, structural inventiveness, and (supposedly) pure geometry. We must therefore look further to explain the inattention of architects, critics, and historians.

To understand what the Arch is not—canonic—we must therefore turn to what it is—iconic. Within months of the competition, and quite spontaneously, the Arch began to be used as a logo by local organizations, public and private, and by local companies, large and small. The practice accelerated powerfully once construction began in 1963. In 1987, one scholar speculated that the Arch had probably gained an "established place in American urban iconography." And so it had, for in that year the Arch was featured in the famous advertising campaign for Absolut Vodka. As "Absolut St. Louis," it was, according to the history of that campaign, a "landmark . . . appreciated and understood . . . by people all over the country," just as Central Park is understood as "Absolut New York," the Brooklyn Bridge as "Absolut Brooklyn," and a Guimard Metro entrance as "Absolut Paris."[12] The Arch functions as an icon of place: it is consensually established and

Absolut St. Louis, one of the series of advertisements created by TBWA for Absolut Vodka. Courtesy of TBWA/Chiat Day.

widely recognized, its image being so realistic that no other indicator of "St. Louis" is necessary.

The Arch is an icon of St. Louis but *only* of St. Louis. Its official federal designation as the Jefferson National Expansion Memorial and the more familiar name of Gateway Arch notwithstanding, the Absolut-ly St. Louisian Arch is not a "national icon," a peer of the Statue of Liberty and Mount Rushmore. Unlike the Statue of Liberty, which manages to be an icon of New York City *and* of the United States, the Arch has never been an icon of the nation, still less of the power of the state. In fact, since 1934, when President Franklin Delano Roosevelt designated the St. Louis Riverfront as a national historical site at the behest of local politicians, both the sincerity and legibility of the monument's commemorative function have been the object of skepticism. In his classic study of the image of Thomas Jefferson, Merrill Peterson observed that "the motivation" for Roosevelt's executive order "seemed to be something less than patriotic, particularly in view of [the fact that the mayor of St. Louis was the former] . . . head of the real estate exchange. But . . . the memorial recommended itself [during the Great Depression] . . . as a relief project."[13] Lauding the Arch to the probably incredulous readers of *Oppositions,* St. Louis novelist-philosopher William Gass has imagined the typical visitor, "the average guy," wondering "what has Jefferson to do with it," but being more interested in "how it was built, in statistics" than in the national history—the westward expansion of the United States following the 1804 Louisiana Purchase by President Jefferson—that the Arch represents. Gass's intuition was later confirmed by a local news reporter, who described the puzzlement of visitors to the Arch's underground museum. They do "not know why it was built until they go inside."[14]

Having argued that the Arch is in no sense a canonic building but rather an icon for local communities, I want to argue more generally that *canon* and *icon* are not synonymous. Historical usage in itself has made the terms distinct. But even if past meanings are ignored and only common modern-day applications—to "exemplary canonical works" and to "icons of popular culture"—are considered, *canon* and *icon* invoke different theoretical domains, different kinds of enemies, and, perhaps most important, different communities of believers—respectively, texts and images, heretics and iconoclasts, critic-historians and students of popular culture. And that is only the beginning. It is unhelpful, to say the least, to use the terms interchangeably in academic discourse.

In architecture, the differences are fundamental. Membership in the canon is conferred by architects through emulation or by critics and historians in their assessment of those architects' written or designed works; iconic stature is conferred by communities of nonarchitects. In short, and simplifying somewhat, canonic works are "made," iconic works "happen."

I submit that most iconic works are not canonic and most canonic works are not iconic, as an examination of several well-known architectural icons of place reveals. To even the playing field, let us exclude from consideration the temples, cathedrals, and capitols that, before being canonic works *or* icons of place, were sites and representations of power. Consider the stature in today's canon of several modern (built after 1750) buildings that, like the Arch, are icons of place: the Eiffel Tower, the Chrysler Building, the Empire State Building, the Sears Tower, the Paris Opera, the Sydney Opera, and, to be up-to-date, the Guggenheim Museum in Bilbao, Spain. In Halbertal's framework, the opera houses are certainly "exemplars of genres," in this case style, and thus are members of the exemplary canon. But they are exemplars with limited significance for the "formative canon" in architecture (although Garnier's Opera is certainly part of the architectural historian's formative canon). Neither Paris nor Sydney is to any significant extent "transmitted or interpreted." To the contrary, while familiarity with Bilbao as part of Frank O. Gehry's oeuvre is a "precondition for membership" in the discipline, the very qualities that make it an icon of Bilbao are precisely those that make it well-nigh impossible for a student to take it up as a "model for imitation." If the other buildings that I have mentioned appear in the survey textbooks, they do so as curiosities or as examples of technical rather than architectural "value and achievement."

In terms of their architectural qualities, what do these icons have in common? The least common denominator is obviousness: superlative tallness in the case of the skyscrapers and literalness of representation in the other cases. An automobile manufacturer's flagship building is topped by a spire resembling a hood ornament and seemingly made of hubcaps; an imperial opera house flourishes a roof-like crown; sail-forming volumes are set on a harbor in a city where sailing is an obsession; and a billowing efflorescence of titanium is intended to recall the flower that is the symbol of the Basque region. Indeed, obviousness is why icons are so easily parodied (irony is harder).

If we can agree that iconic buildings are characteristically common and ordinary, and that canonic buildings are unique and rare, then we can turn to Bourdieu for help in understanding what is at stake socially in such seemingly natural and obvious categories.[15] In *Distinction: A Social Critique of the Judgement of Taste*, Bourdieu maintains that pairs of these very adjectives—common/unique, ordinary/rare—and others like them are manifestations of matrix-like schemas of perception that work to "classify and qualify persons and objects in the most varied areas of practice," precisely because such paired oppositions are themselves produced by the fundamental social division of any social group into "dominant" and "dominated" classes.[16]

These classifications, Bourdieu claims, are wrongly considered to be simply aesthetic categories. Refuting traditional aesthetic philosophy, he maintains that such categories operate in all domains of social activity and not merely in those of culture and art, that they are social (the result of personal and collective history) and not universal, and that they are relational (that is, meaningful only in relation to each other, "high" naturally conjuring up "low" even when "low" has not been mentioned) and not pure or ideal. Correspondingly, "taste" is a manifestation of a preference for anything, in any domain; it is expressed in all individual or group activities, or what Bourdieu calls "practices," and is never inherently good or bad, only perceived as such in relationship to others' tastes, which are also expressed in practices. It follows that not only do taste preferences classify things, they also classify those who own or lack them. Moreover, the social being the relational, taste preferences classify the classifier, uniting an individual and member of a group with some people and groups and differentiating him or her from others.

It is important to see how this occurs. Categories such as common/unique are the outward expression of schemas of "perception and appreciation" that are themselves invisible, working below the radar screen of consciousness. These schemas are part of what Bourdieu calls the "habitus." The habitus is often described as a "practical sense," a "second nature," or a "feel for the game" of the kind possessed by a highly skilled athlete. (In his youth, Bourdieu was a serious rugby player.) It incorporates (in the sense that it embodies) the knowledge and experience gained by living in society and its sub-groups, includes both material *and* symbolic conditions of existence, and is initially formed in the ambit of the family and the school, be-cause it is there that we are socialized. The special skills of the disci-plines and "professions" (a term Bourdieu eschews) are incorporated later in life and constitute what he calls a "cognitive habitus."

The habitus, as Bourdieu frequently puts it, is "history embodied," but it should not be mistaken for "destiny," for two reasons. First, the habitus constantly accumulates and reacts to experiential knowledge; second, it conditions but does not determine choices. The habitus op-erates within and through schemas, and these schemas orient what we commonly call our taste—preferences in music, architecture and art, dresses, ties, and cars—and our lifestyle—manners, posture, gait, and choice of spouses and friends, everything that makes us feel comfortable in certain worlds and uncomfortable in others, or what Bourdieu calls "a sense of one's place."

Lifestyles, the "systematic products" of the habitus, become "sign systems that are socially qualified . . . as 'distinguished' [or] 'vulgar' but only when perceived in their mutual relations through the sche-mas of the habitus," one's own and others'.[17] The aspect of lifestyle and taste that particularly concerns us is what Bourdieu terms the "aesthetic disposition," the disposition that characterizes those pos-sessing "distinction." Obviously, the material conditions of the domi-nant and dominated differ. Equally obviously, trying to earn enough to live on is the primary material condition of the dominated, bring-ing with it necessity and constraint. The members of the dominated class—exemplified by the French working class that Bourdieu and his team surveyed—experience their taste and lifestyles as the expression of free choices and preferences, but in fact their taste and lifestyles are predicated on an initial condition of necessity. In this way, ac-cording to Bourdieu, the habitus can make a virtue out of necessity, and he captures that paradox in the phrase "a taste for necessity." Among those surveyed, this taste was manifest on the one hand in a preference for things that are functional, and on the other by an unconstrained hedonism in eating or drinking, and for lively, playful language.

Taste being social and relational, the opposite of a "taste for ne-cessity" is naturally "a taste for freedom." The more distant one is from the tastes and lifestyles of those with the habitus of the domi-nated, the freer one is, the more distinguished one is—distinction in

French signifying both being "distinct from others" and being *distin-gué*. Possession of an "aesthetic disposition" is typical of individuals who possess such freedom. Fundamental to the aesthetic disposition is a distancing from "what is generic, *common*, 'easy' and immediately accessible . . . the content of the representation," and a preference for the abstract and the difficult that require the deciphering of "meaningful signs."[18]

Although my reading of Bourdieu's *Distinction* is admittedly selective (and there is much more in his sociology of relevance to architecture), its relevance to the subject of icons and canons should now be clear. The qualities of obviousness identified as the least common denominator of iconicity in architecture are precisely those abhorred by those of an aesthetic disposition. Canonic works, on the other hand, demand decoding because they encode links to previous works in the form of signs usually intelligible only to other makers and to authorities on that making. Remembering Halbertal, we can conclude that if the formative canon is a "cultural asset" for a "society or profession," then the icon is a cultural asset for which no formation is required. All iconic persons or objects become iconic without the benefit of being deliberately taught, transmitted, and interpreted; knowledge of them is not essential to, nor does it convey, membership in a restricted group, let alone establish one as possessing distinguishing taste. Discerning and comprehending canonical works, conversely, require the skills and knowledge that come with membership in a discipline, because the formative canon constitutes its home and core, the initiation and the modalities of professional socialization.

Interest in the applicability of Bourdieu's sociology to architecture is on the rise, as the summer 2000 edition of *Harvard Design Magazine,* on "design and class," suggests. There has yet, however, to be any full-scale sociological investigation into populations of architects or architects-in-training that even remotely resembles the one that undergirds *Distinction*.[19] Such a survey would be needed to demonstrate empirically that a disdain for iconic buildings is inculcated in architectural education along with, and as the distinguishing "other" to, a respect for canonic buildings. In its absence, I submit that the silence surrounding the iconic Arch demonstrates that such inculcation does somehow occur and that Bourdieu's notion of the "aesthetic disposition" gives us a sociological and philosophical explanation of why icons elicit disdain.

Just how difficult it is for us to admire an icon can be observed in the one account of the Arch by an architect, and a prominent architect at that. In an interview in the Japanese journal *A+U*, Robert Venturi responded to editor Tsukasa Yamashita's request to identify his preferred work by Saarinen, his former employer. Venturi first speaks about the Arch from what might be termed the eyewitness point of view. "Speaking very, very quickly, making a quick decision, I would have to say that the St. Louis Arch was very impressive. I saw it recently again. . . . The fact that it happened is wonderful and I think that the design of it is very, very beautiful . . . [with its] kind of a magical scaleless quality . . . an ambiguity; you never know how big it is, how far away it is; it's structurally present and has a distinct symbolism, being [either] a door or an entrance. . . . It has a very directional quality. It is very different from the [West and East] than it is from the North [and South]. It's very rich. . . . You can look at it many ways."

Venturi's second point of view resembles that of the expert witness, invoking history, professional know-how, and criteria of quality and difficulty in order to rank the work among other works. "One of the best things, one of the best things since World War II . . . a thing that is very difficult to do, which is a non-functional, sculptural, symbolic gesture of enormous scale. . . . It has many qualities, and that means that it is very good. . . . So I think it is the most impressive thing that [Saarinen] did, except it's not a building. . . . It is very much of its time, kind of a great structural gesture showing off the technological structural abilities. I think that it is one of the best things that's ever been done."[20]

Venturi's words and thoughts here are unlike those that precede and follow them in the lengthy interview, in which he expressed unqualified praise for Saarinen's professionalism and "styles-for-the-job" approach, as well as more qualified estimations of his talent as a designer. As if to undercut the idea floated elsewhere in the magazine that he is a "son" of Saarinen, Venturi declares that Jean Labatut and Louis Kahn were his true "masters."[21] Let Freudians speculate as they will, the discussion of the Arch follows immediately upon this possible symbolic patricide.

"Denial," however, is the least of Venturi's infractions. Greater still is his crime of *lèse catégorie*. Venturi effects a double rupture from the canon, for he both apprehends the Arch as an icon and proposes its canonization. First, the icon: The eyewitness Venturi is viewing the Arch with *both* the astonished gaze of the first-time visitor ("very impressive") *and* with the experienced one of a St. Louisian who has observed its diversity ("you can look at it many ways"). His professional vocabulary and categories of classification ("difficult" and "of its time") are leavened with the language, rhetoric, and, most important, criteria of those who esteem the Arch as an icon. Speaking in what Ludwig Wittgenstein calls "ordinary language" ("wonderful," "magical") and repeatedly making hyperbolic claims ("the best"), he sees the Arch as something that has happened, something received or imposed, and not solely as an artifact designed by an architect. And, like the ordinary citizens of St. Louis, he believes that it is wonderful that the Arch was built. Second, the canonization: The Arch is the best of its class ("since World War II") and the best of show ("ever been done"). Yet the Arch is "not a building," presumably because it is "non-functional." This is surely canonization with a caveat.[22]

On the face of it, Venturi has provided an answer to the puzzle of the Arch's continued exclusion from the canon. It is not a building, and the canon is limited to buildings. Venturi's view is not idiosyncratic. It is shared by other "Saarinen grads" interviewed by *A+U*. Cesar Pelli describes it as "not a building with many utilitarian things." For Anthony Lumsden, it is a building, but "a little like" the Statue of Liberty, in being "probably not functional." The American Institute of Architects was of the same opinion, calling the Arch an object that "had no other purpose than to portray, promote or symbolize an idea of high spiritual concern." Moreover, much like Venturi, both Pelli and Lumsden connect lack of function with iconicity. For Pelli, the Arch is "pure and simple, [which] . . . was the strongest image always." Lumsden speculates that "it's probably done a lot for the people of St. Louis . . . given some focus and recognition."[23]

We could stop there, but Bourdieu emboldens us to go further, to consider Venturi's testimony in terms of those "unconscious presuppositions" about which he warned us. Venturi's reading reveals how the Arch both highlights and confuses many of the categories specific to the discipline of architecture. Architectural typologies fail to work or even to matter in the case of the Arch. It is part of a building ("a door") and bears the name of a doorway, but it is said to be neither a building nor functional. Similarly, professional and disciplinary distinctions also collapse when confronted with the Arch. It is "structural," implying that it is the work of an architect or an engineer, and "sculptural," a word that conjures up the artist. The Arch also throws into question the measurement of quality and achievement in architecture, for a nonbuilding is declared a "very difficult thing to do" and wins the prize of "best ever."

The Arch confuses the categories of the classified as well. It should come as no surprise that Venturi, a member of the team who Learned from Las Vegas and Levittown, is able to look at the Arch from the viewpoint of a St. Louisian. The Arch also serves his (probably unconscious) purpose well. Its richness confirms what is probably the subtext of the interview—that pluralism is the only quality he shares with Saarinen. Nonetheless, when local knowledge gained from reading is made the equal of professional knowledge acquired through training, when the expert witness and the eyewitness speak in the same voice, when the canonizer sees with the gaze of the admirer of icons and categorizes architecture as something "that happens"— when this occurs, an unholy mixture of aesthetic categories and "aesthetic dispositions" has been concocted. Venturi's recourse to the caveat ("not a building") is understandable, for it restores categorical distinctions and, with them, "aesthetic dispositions." (His final "best ever" would then be a Galileo-like recanting of his recanting, a "yet [the earth] moves.")

As was the case for *A+U* editor and interviewer Yamashita, whose enthusiasm for the Arch arose during a teaching stint in Missouri, it is repeated visits that apparently allowed Venturi to see the Arch that has remained invisible to so many others. It is striking to compare Venturi's assessment with that of George McCue. Although from a Bourdieuean point of view, a music critic like McCue is no ordinary St. Louisian, McCue was self-taught in architecture, and his description of the Arch captures what I have heard many St. Louisians say. Like them, he describes how "it is visible for more than thirty miles from the Illinois hilltops and highways"; how on the Missouri side, where hilly terrain limits viewing, the Arch can reveal itself "by a sudden flashing of the sun on the summit curve"; how one looks "across the roof of a warehouse, or at the end of a row of alleys, or high above industrial chimneys, [and] suddenly, there it is"; and finally, how it takes on different hues and even turns black.[24]

Although the possibility that this mode of apprehension is itself the result of "clandestine persuasion" cannot be excluded, texts that describe the Arch in aesthetic terms are few and far between. Scholars have primarily cast the Arch as either the forerunner of city-destroying urban renewal or as a hegemonic national monument to western expansion whose form suitably recalls ancient imperialism.

Aesthetic evaluations such as McCue's and Gass's were not cited and Meyerowitz's photographs were not reproduced in the two television specials that celebrated the Arch's twenty-fifth anniversary. Moreover, advice on viewing the structure is not included in the standard guidebooks to St. Louis architecture. Given all that, along with the Arch's "immediate accessibility . . . [as] the thing represented," it just may be that the Arch's iconicity enables St. Louisians to enjoy an "artistic experience shorn of ritualism and exhibitionism"[25] and that an "aesthetic" appreciation of how the Arch plays hide-and-seek and changes its skin is common currency, "ordinary" knowledge, acquired while doing and not while gazing aesthetically.

The case has been made here for the existence of "imposed . . . unconscious suppositions" that have had the effect of "clandestine persuasion" in "texts" intended for and written by "readers," even among those predisposed to view Saarinen's work favorably. The Arch's "immediate accessibility" has certainly worked to the disadvantage of professional readers, the Saarinen graduates among them. They believed that because the Arch lacks function, it is "simple," when in fact it is anything but simple.

What then are the lessons to be learned from St. Louis, other than that the Arch merits the journey (to evoke the *Michelin Guide*'s highest ranking), preferably in the company of a "native guide"?

Those who would argue that there is no getting away from canons because canons are formative can find comfort and confirmation in both Halbertal's and Bourdieu's arguments. If there is no canon, there is no architecture—or any other profession or discipline, for that matter. But the upholders of canons must also consider the implications of this. Bourdieu notes that "cultivated men [sic] . . . may have different opinions on the subjects about which they quarrel, but they are . . . agreed on quarreling about certain subjects."[26] Canon expansion, explosion, and even implosion—a word that recalls the Jencksian view that the destruction of St. Louis's Pruitt-Igoe Modernist public housing signaled the demise of Modernism—are *all* forms of canonization; they just follow different trajectories.

Much can be gained from introducing icons into our teaching and into the lifelong learning of architecture culture—introduced as irritants to the canon and not as its stepchildren. Icons should form the limiting cases that make us think about the categories that undergird canonical thinking and that are embedded in "aesthetic dispositions." If done honestly—that is, through the historicization of which Bourdieu speaks—then the teaching of icons would include the history of their exclusion from history, thereby bringing to light the darker distinguishing side of canonical belief that does harm to people—makers and readers alike—by doing harm to the reputations of buildings.

Although we cannot do away with canons, an understanding of their "social history" can at least limit their collateral damage. Saarinen, who was so often "rejected and derided" that mention of this was made in his obituaries, knew how discriminatory the discriminating can be. So does Venturi, whose social origins were mocked as part of the "critical evaluation" by the British press of his addition to the National Gallery. Confronting the canon with icons brings categorization to consciousness, and consciousness of categorization is the first step toward emancipation from the categories we impose upon ourselves as well as others when we classify things.

2001

Notes

1. Father Joseph Faherty, Joe Mason, and the members of the Arteaga family are interviewed in *Gateway Arch Silver Anniversary,* Julius Hunter and Laurie Connors (KMOV, 1990), videotape, courtesy of the Missouri Historical Society; George McCue, "The Arch: An Appreciation," *AIA Journal,* November 1978, 62; Joel Meyerowitz, *St. Louis and the Arch: Photographs by Joel Meyerowitz,* with a preface by James Wood (Boston: New York Graphic Society, 1980), 10; Pierre Bourdieu and Loïc J. D. Wacquant, *An Invitation to Reflexive Sociology* (Chicago: University of Chicago Press, 1992), 87. For the history of the Arch's creation, see Hélène Lipstadt, "Lokale Kontra Nationale Erinnerung: Kollektives Gedenken, Kollektive Erinnerung und der Gateway Arch," *Denkmale und Kulturelles Gedächtnis Nach dem Ende der Ost-West-Konfrontation* (Berlin: Akademie der Künste/Jovis Verlag, 2000), 101–12, a synopsis of a chapter from the book on Modernism and American twentieth-century monuments that this writer is preparing. Support for research on the Arch received from the Missouri Historical Society and the Graham Foundation for Advanced Study in the Fine Arts is gratefully acknowledged. I also thank Cathy Corbett, Andrew Hurley, Eric Mumford, Van Reidhead, Eric Sandweiss, and John Wolfert for discussing St. Louisians' attitudes to the Arch with me, and *Harvard Design Magazine* editors William Saunders and Nancy Levinson for their challenging response to a first draft of this article.

2. Rosalind Krauss, "Sculpture in the Expanded Field," *The Art of Art History: A Critical Anthology,* ed. Donald Preziosi (New York: Oxford University Press, 1998), 294–95; James Young, "Memory and Counter-Memory," *Harvard Design Magazine,* Fall 1999, 4–13. For further discussion of counter-monuments, see Hélène Lipstadt, "Memoryware," *Assemblage* 41, 45.

3. As quoted in Michael Payne, "Canon," in *A Dictionary of Cultural and Critical Theory,* ed. Michael Payne (Oxford: Blackwell, 1996), 91.

4. Reyner Banham, *Age of the Masters: A Personal View of Modern Architecture* (New York: Harper & Row, 1975), 12; Herbert Muschamp, "It's History Now, So Shouldn't Modernism Be Preserved, Too?" *New York Times,* December 17, 2000, Arts and Leisure, 40.

5. Pierre Bourdieu and Roger Chartier, *Pratiques de la lecture,* ed. Roger Chartier (Marseilles: Rivages, 1985), 220, 238, 218, 219. Regrettably, I learned of John Guillory, *Cultural Capital: The Problem of Literary Canon Formation* (Chicago: University of Chicago Press, 1993) too late to use in this article.

6. Paul Kennon and Tsukasa Yamashita, "Interviewee 6: Paul Kennon," *A+U: Eero Saarinen and His Works* (April 1984): 236; Cesar Pelli and Tsukasa Yamashita, "Interviewee 4: Cesar Pelli," *A+U: Eero Saarinen,* 229; Paul Heyer, *Architects on Architecture: New Directions in America* (New York: Walker and Company, 1978), 351.

7. John Jacobus, *Twentieth-Century Architecture: The Middle Years, 1940–1965* (New York: Frederick A. Praeger, 1966), 112; Reyner Banham, *Guide to Modern Architecture* (London: Architectural Press, 1962), 112–13.

8. Lawrence Lessing, "The Diversity of Eero Saarinen," *Architectural Forum,* July 1960, 94–103; Banham, *Age of the Masters,* 122.

9. Vincent Scully, *American Architecture and Urbanism* (New York: Praeger, 1969), 196.

10. The most notable and valuable exception is that of Peter Papademetriou, "Coming of Age: Eero Saarinen and Modern American Architecture," *Perspecta* 21 (1984): 116–41; but even in this exemplary article, the Arch receives only a single page of attention.

11. All quotations that follow in this paragraph are from Moshe Halbertal, *People of the Book: Canon, Meaning, Authority* (Cambridge, Mass.: Harvard University Press, 1997), 3–4.

12. Patricia Raub, "The Making of an Urban Landmark: Media Images of the St. Louis Gateway Arch," *Gateway Heritage,* Winter 1987–88, 46; Richard W. Lewis, *Absolut Book: The Absolut Vodka Advertising Story* (Boston: Journey Editions, 1996), 48, 59, 56.

13. Albert Boime, *The Unveiling of the National Icons: A Plea for Patriotic Iconoclasm in a Nationalist Era* (Cambridge: Cambridge University

Press, 1998), 1; Merrill D. Peterson, *The Jefferson Image in the American Mind* (New York: Oxford University Press, 1962), 423.

14. William H. Gass, "Monumentality/Mentality," *Oppositions* 24 (Fall 1982): 138; *Gateway Arch Silver Anniversary.*

15. Bourdieu can be applied to architecture more generally; see Hélène Lipstadt, "Theorizing the Competition: The Sociology of Pierre Bourdieu as a Challenge to Architectural History," *Thresholds* 21 (2000): 23–36.

16. Pierre Bourdieu, *Distinction: A Social Critique of the Judgement of Taste* (Cambridge, Mass.: Harvard University Press, 1984), 468, 546, 468.

17. Ibid., 172.

18. Ibid., 172, 32, 499.

19. This is not the place for a bibliographic review, nor, given the explosion of interest in Bourdieu in the American academy in the past five years, is it the time, for more examinations are surely to appear. The author hopes that the failing that has until recently prevailed in the United States, that of approaching Bourdieu piecemeal—using the notion of cultural capital without that of the habitus, or applying Bourdieu's early work on museums without taking into account his later work on the artistic gaze, for example—will not be repeated.

20. Venturi actually says North and South—that is, viewed when parallel to the Arch—which makes no sense. My interpolation reflects the fact that he is responding to the interviewer's suggestion that the Arch looks different when viewed on the east-west axis, that is, frontally, than it does when one is "paralleling the river, [when] it appears just like a tower, like the Washington Monument." Robert Venturi and Tsukasa Yamashita, "Interviewee 2: Robert Venturi," *A+U: Eero Saarinen,* 220.

21. Venturi and Yamashita, *A+U: Eero Saarinen,* 228.

22. I leave to specialists the task of squaring the famed Venturi and Scott Brown duck/decorated shed distinction with this assessment of the doorlike (and thus ducklike?) Arch, or Venturi's doctrine of complexity and contradiction with his upholding of the Modernist orthodoxy of function as the essential condition of buildingness.

23. Pelli and Yamashita, *A+U: Eero Saarinen,* 226; Anthony Lumsden and Tsukasa Yamashita, "Interviewee 5: Anthony Lumsden," *A+U: Eero Saarinen,* 233; Aline Saarinen, "A Message from Aline Saarinen," *AIA Journal,* September 1966, 68.

24. Mason, cited in McCue, "The Arch," 58, 62.

25. Bourdieu, cited in Bourdieu and Wacquant, *An Invitation to Reflexive Sociology,* 87.

26. Pierre Bourdieu, "Intellectual Field and Creative Project," in *Knowledge and Control: New Directions for the Sociology of Education,* ed. M. F. D. Young (London: Collier-Macmillan, 1971), 182–83.

2

What Goes Unnoticed: On the Canonical Quality of the PSFS Building

David Leatherbarrow

While paradoxical, it is nonetheless true that the buildings that merit continued study and interest, decade after decade, are those that do not insist on our attention in everyday experience. Put more strongly: works of very high rank—canonical works—are precisely those that ordinarily go unnoticed. These works sustain wonder but do not demand it. When one of my students admitted with embarrassment that he had often walked by such a building—the Philadelphia Saving Fund Society Building, or PSFS Building, in Philadelphia—and failed to notice it (although I had shown it in class), I explained that his neglect may not have displeased its architects.[1] They thought that as "an outward expression of the contemporary life process,"[2] a building's first task is to play its part in the workings of a street, block, and city, giving the patterns of contemporary life durable dimension, suitable enclosure, and expression. Le Corbusier, whose ideas George Howe, one of the building's designers, often invoked, stressed unobtrusiveness when characterizing furnishings: a chair, like "a good servant[,] is discreet and self-effacing, in order to leave his master free."[3] Great buildings, too, are alternately expressive and recessive, remarkably beautiful and unpronounced. In this way also they both transcend common sense and assume it.

By definition, canonical works are those that establish a standard or norm according to which others can be measured. Such a work is at once an instrument of measure and a criterion of judgment. A *canon* could thus be a list of exemplary texts on a given subject, a recurring musical motif, or a statement of policy, public or ecclesiastical. Further, and closer to the ancient Greek senses of the term, a canon could be the top horizontal beam of a loom (or its shuttle), the tongue or beam of a balance, the crossbar of a lyre, or the stops of a flute. Each of these sets a standard for measurement. In archaic usage, canon named the bars in the hollow of a warrior's shield by which it was held up in the right position. Taken in aggregate, these objects indicate something that is straight, unbending or unyielding, and consequently useful as a measure, not of length but of outer shape or edge profile. Hence, the expression "true to the canon" intends perfect alignment or conformity to something taken to be right. *Justification* in building construction and graphic design intends the same thing. In the records of the building of the Erechtheion in Athens, there is a description of a typical finishing canon used by builders as a shaping and scraping instrument, a straightedge that measured twenty feet long, six inches wide, and about five inches deep. Like the so-called Doric norm, it was absolutely rigid and perfectly true. Scraped away with this instrument were not only irregularities but also particularities.

Canonical works of architecture are thus those we take to be very good—so good they can be used as a guide to gauge the merit of other works. The "we" of this statement is not simple, however, for it refers to at least three distinct sources of evaluation: society at large, the discipline itself (including the experience and knowledge of both professionals and professors), and any particular individual's interests. Agreement about what is good is no more common than disagreement among these groups; what professionals take to be exemplary often differs from what professors take to be canonical, and likewise for the examples selected by clients and critics. In fact, the mere mention of anything like a norm or standard instantly prompts a fairly blunt question: "Whose?" Confronting this question, one might wish to drop the issue altogether, but that does not overcome or alleviate the difficulty of making judgments in either criticism or design. At the outset, I would like to suspend the question about whose canon is superior because one of my concerns is to see how the professors and the public might agree and disagree, how disciplinary and circumstantial norms might relate to one another. Yet the matter is even more difficult because the determination of standards by each of these agents will vary over time; more than likely yesterday's canon will be neither today's nor tomorrow's. Hence the need for periodic reevaluation, reevaluation that tends toward rejection or reaffirmation, depending on what has changed and what has remained the same.

"From the time a building is completed its destruction begins."[4] So wrote Frederick Gutheim in his 1949 reappraisal of the Philadelphia Saving Fund Society Building, which has been described as the most important tall building built in the United States in the period between Louis Sullivan's skyscrapers in Chicago and Mies van der Rohe's Seagram Building in New York.[5] It was designed by George Howe and William Lescaze and built between 1929 and 1932. Gutheim concluded his reassessment of the PSFS Building by reflecting broadly on the continuity and continued relevance of buildings. He observed that the uses for which buildings are designed begin to change shortly after the occupants move in. Once begun, this sort of change is continual. A similar observation led Aldo Rossi to his famous critique of naive functionalism—inconstant functions are an inadequate basis for architectural permanence—and his turn toward architecture's "immutable principles."[6] The matter is not only theoretical, for once the original furnishings and settings fail to accommodate new needs—and fail they eventually will—alteration or substitution will soon follow. Every building's life story is a tale of loss, every construction suffers continual and increasing modification, a fate to which the tears of historic preservationists testify.

The process of adapting or adjusting a building to new needs merits additional thought because this activity is always based on some measure of reappraisal, not of the sort that critics undertake, according to a professional or professorial canon, but instead according to a practical standard applied to immediate concerns. While architects and critics may find this an inferior sort of assessment, because unprofessional, it is nonetheless keenly observant of contemporary interests, and its proposals are often ingenious. Further, practical reappraisals harbor their own standards of what ought to be, and they are no less firmly held than are those of professionals. Yet they are impermanent because they pertain to particular buildings, not to "architecture." Despite the concreteness, intelligence, and inevitability of this nonprofessional sort of appraisal and alteration, Gutheim lamented it, for the cumulative effect of modification inevitably leads to the loss of something on which he thought greatness in architec-

PSFS Building, circa 1930s. Photograph by Richard Dooner. Courtesy of Hagley Museum and Library.

ture depends: wholeness or unity, that interdependency of parts or coherence that makes a building, like a living thing, *organic*.

A related commonplace is that buildings with organic unity are those that have *style*. Such was the opinion of Gutheim, for one, but also of George Howe and William Lescaze, and, of course, of Frank

Lloyd Wright. The history of this conceit hardly begins there, however, for as Edward De Zurko demonstrated in *Origins of Functionalist Theory*, there was a prehistory of Modernist ideas on organic order and style in the eighteenth and nineteenth centuries. More recently, Caroline van Eck, in *Organicism in Nineteenth-Century Architecture*, has pointed to antecedents for these ideas in the early Renaissance and antiquity, referring to wholeness or unity in both built and rhetorical works. In the arguments she studies, as in those described by De Zurko, disturbances to organic unity were thought to compromise internal definition, and with it style. This was also Gutheim's position.

But is style important in determining the meaning and importance of a work of architecture, even its canonical status? In the literature on the PSFS Building, there are many attempts at identifying its style and its place in the grand history of styles. All the effort spent on locating and identifying precedents for its formal motifs is part of this attempt. The historians who have contributed most to our understanding of the building, William Jordy and Robert Stern, have worked hard at this, making comparisons between the PSFS Building and examples from European Modernism and the Beaux-Arts tradition. In their concern with motifs and style, they followed the two who put the building in the center of the debate on the International Style, Henry-Russell Hitchcock and Philip Johnson, who included it in the famous Museum of Modern Art exhibition of 1932 and the book that followed. This interest has not diminished in recent years, for the promotions department of the building's new occupant, Loews Hotel, has taken up the question once again, describing the building as an Art Deco masterpiece.[7] While unending, which is to say inconclusive, this approach is not particularly wrongheaded, but it does, I think, raise a question: Does the identification of a building's style or its formal precedents help us understand its contemporary and continued importance, in either architectural design or everyday life? Here I turn from the canons of the history professors to the measures of quality recognized by both architects and the public. This distinction can take the form of a question. Is a building "canonical" because its motifs have been composed to perfectly exemplify a style, because it is a singularly eloquent example of a particular kind of expression and thus entitled to a place in the history of styles, or is a building such as the PSFS important because its primary order still makes sense as part of a street, a block, and a city, despite changes in society and its institutions?

Gutheim believed that the loss of style, through the gradual alteration of a building's elements and settings, would result in anonymity. Like the sinking of the *Titanic*, the beginning of such an end is
disarmingly discreet: "The process begins most easily with decoration and other elusive details. In older buildings it spreads to store
fronts, lighting fixtures, elevator cabs, lobbies, corridors, and their
very facades. Advanced stages are signalized by major reconstruc-
tions. Hardly one of these individual changes can be objected to with
any force, but their cumulative effect leads to anonymity."[8]

In the case of the PSFS Building, this process started with changes
in the banking room, particularly the removal of countertop lights
and the installation of ceiling illumination. The erosion of unity continued with changes to the furnishings, then to the shops below, the
connection to the subway, and so on. The recent changes that were
made to accommodate the hotel that has replaced the bank have
greatly accelerated the movement toward "anonymity." For Gutheim,
as I have said, this was a problem. It is also a problem for some preservationists, or more exactly for "antipreservationists" who advo-
cate "restoration," the outcome of which, I think, is what Aldo Rossi
meant by "pathological permanence." Yet this building was and has
remained a living part of its street, block, and city—configurations
not made up of buildings that are noticeably stylish but rather of
more or less inconspicuous buildings that serve as the "background"
for contemporary life. In our concern with distinctive imagery, have
we forgotten this modest but decisive role of buildings? Because of
the ways it plays a part in such a background, a building might use-
fully and positively be described as *anonymous*—so much a part of
life that it recedes from one's attention. This is true, I think, for the
PSFS Building, even with its history of local modifications. Yet this
building's adherence to its street and city did not result from any sort
of mimicry of nearby motifs or conditions; if anything, it was vividly
distinct when it was built. Its discordance was the kind that proposed
some conditions while recalling others: cantilevers in the first case,
and bay windows in the second. It cannot be considered as distinct
from its vicinity, if that distinctiveness is thought to result from the
sort of internal definition (organic unity) that assumes conceptual
and practical autonomy, for little of the PSFS can be understood if
one neglects its particular location and the institutional practices it
was meant to house. If this building is unified in its internal definition, it is so with respect to all that is outside it, as if building and

site were part and counterpart. What is more, its manner of engaging its milieu—reinterpreting and reforming some of the city's typical situations—has allowed it to respond to changes in that milieu and to changes in its own makeup, as if its finality in 1932 were essentially provisional, as if its "unity" were purposely incomplete, always still to be realized. While this is an outrage for proponents of style history and of organic theory, perhaps here we have a characteristic of canonical works that can be added to their "unobtrusive beauty": that their responsive and productive engagement with the situations and settings of their vicinity gives the unity they possess sufficient openness to sustain continual redefinition. For such a building, time is not a threat but a partial memory and a spectrum of unforeseen opportunity.

The PSFS Building has been neglected somewhat in the history of modern architecture. According to Gutheim, this was because it was "not new enough to be contemporary" and "not old enough to have become a readily placed historical monument." Furthermore, it was a building that, according to Stern, still carried traces of the earlier Beaux-Arts tradition of design,[9] despite its prominent position in Hitchcock and Johnson's *The International Style*. This ambiguity is also reflected in the fact that the building was seen by many to be "ultramodern," but its owner understood its design to result from practical considerations. Practicality was wedded to a "look" that expressed progressive thinking. The same coupling of tradition and modernity can be seen in the relationship between the building's two architects: Howe represented the best of tradition, and Lescaze brought to the project the momentum of European Modernism. Both were necessary in dealing with the client, who was himself a product of traditional upbringing but also aware that cultural conditions were no longer the same.

The building was designed to be "ultrapractical." This term has been credited to James Wilcox, the president of the Philadelphia Saving Fund Society and the architects' client. Initially, it can be understood in two senses, programmatic and technological. Under the heading of the first sort of practicality, much has been written about the novelty and foresight of placing the commercial and public banking facilities on the building's second floor, above street level, reached by a stairway or the famous escalator. While controversial, because uncommon, this decision proved to have great practical advantage, for it left the ground level free for retail activities, which at-

PSFS Building, now Loews Hotel, circa 2000. Copyright Jeff Goldberg/Esto.

tracted into the bank potential customers who might not have entered the building were those other uses not there—as was the case with the Fidelity Trust building newly completed a few blocks away on Broad Street, described by Howe as a "notorious failure." The design of the PSFS Building might thus be described as practical urbanism. And its practicality was also technological. This was apparent in its distribution of interior settings and the elements that accommodated their use—those that provided for day lighting, for example, but also for thermal comfort. These characteristics were as much the result of the asymmetrical additive arrangement of the building's overall volumes, responding to local site conditions, as of its equipment and mechanical parts. The PSFS Building was the second high-rise in the United States to be fully air-conditioned. Program and use were not made to conform to the logic of an idealized structural frame or diagram of functions (for example, a common circulation core with perimeter offices) but were taken as the basis for differentiating pragmatically determined volumes on the southwest corner of an urban block. While compromising its formal ideality, this attention to particularity of site and use allowed its owner, architects, and apologists to describe the building as "ultrapractical."

Yet practicality is no simple issue in architecture, especially when the aim of a project is *ultra*practicality. What might this term have meant? Was *ultra* thought to be a matter of increase, meaning that ultrapractical is *extremely* practical, or could it indicate architectural conditions that are somehow "beyond" the practical? If so, what might they be? Surely not matters of expediency, efficiency, or need-based functionality. The use of materials inside the building has been described as "refinement approaching over-refinement."[10] Could this and similar statements that testify to a sense of surplus indicate a condition of "practicality" that was essentially qualitative? Could it mean that the things themselves were one of the concerns of the architects, not only their serviceability? Howe suggested this, arguing in 1932 that "functionalism" was not only a practical but also an "aesthetic" issue.[11] But while aesthetic issues were concerns of appearance, image, and beauty, their means of realization—simplicity, refinement, economy—were also characteristic of practical affairs, as if the building's profiles indicated the bank's practices.

Consider the famous banking room. Not long after the building was finished, a new lighting system was installed. One can assume that the illumination from recessed and indirect lighting together with the broad sweep of perimeter glazing facing north and east was found to be inadequate from a strictly functional point of view, although one suspects that the room would have seemed bright when first built. Jordy, not intending dispraise, described the interior as "subdued" and "shadowy." More encouragingly, he introduced the term "muted splendor" to define the quality of the interior finishes. Gutheim had a parallel observation about the building's beauty—it was "a curious, haunting and distinctive kind of beauty" in which muted tones, shadows, and the play of reflections had their part. These terms suggest, and early photographs confirm, that the original condition of the room, while not practical by our standards, because a little dim, was not without aesthetic quality. Of those who reported on it, all were impressed by its *dignity*. It seems to me that this characteristic, difficult as it may be to define, is what still invites thought, not the building's style.

Jordy implied that the building's qualities resulted not from rejection of ornament but from a manner of construction or style of detailing, the result of which was "laconic precision." He did not elaborate the point, but the characteristics of the construction are apparent. Throughout the building, joints between any two elements are not covered by a third element, as they would typically have been in traditional detailing, nor are they kept slightly apart, so as to form a reveal, as in more recent detailing; instead, they are butted together, the consequence of which is uninterrupted planarity. This quality is reinforced by the use of many elements in series: ribbon windows made out of a series of single units, repetitive cladding panels (inside and out), aligned bays of mechanical equipment and furnishings, recessed and concealed light sources. Repetition in these instances does not seem to have been a matter of expediency or of cost cutting but a means toward a specific and specifically qualitative end. The treatment of the building's surfaces, inside and out, works toward the same goal of laconic precision, or a kind of muted splendor. Little or nothing is applied to the building's materials—neither paper nor paint. Instead each piece of steel or stone is polished to a specified degree. This gives each setting a specific temperature: matte finishes and variegated material color in (warm) social spaces, and high polish on uniformly colored materials in (cooler) business settings. Representation is thus avoided, and the things themselves are exposed. Dark opacity is not all that results, for high polish leads to both absorption and reflection, particularly when opaque surfaces are adjacent to those that are transparent or translucent. Think of each panel of black stone as a delta into and onto which flow patterns of light and geometry from the most distant reaches of the urban landscape, but never ceasing to flow, never leaving a durable trace on the black, having marked it for just a while. That the building's artificial lighting is almost always hidden allows its illumination to play off these surfaces, augmenting and reflecting their several qualities from one plane to another.

Is Jordy correct in pointing to construction and finishing when explaining the building's "extra" functional qualities? Surely nothing is so effective in giving the building its shadowy kind of beauty than its palpable body. Is this not also what makes its "laconic" space "haunting," what gives it such a strong sense of emptiness or loss, of readiness to receive? The room, like the bank, is a receptacle; its large dimension, or great capacity, like its silent surfaces and its colorless, limpid light, restrains all qualities other than those that indicate readiness to receive. One conclusion to this line of thinking could be that these qualities result from the scraping away of particularities of circumstance and conventional motif. But the opposite is also true: that the procedure of elimination or distillation gives one the sense of anticipation, of potential, of something about to occur. On this account, it would seem that the architects were content to let the settings wait, to anticipate possible forms of occupation. The purpose of the settings is not to indicate or to show but to remain incomplete in themselves, empty of indication but full of potential.

What is the relationship between this potentiality and the raw or uncompromising rationality that we tend to associate with functionalism? Do both contribute to style? How could this be, when functionalism was conceived by many to be the "style" that would end all styles, when anonymity was not a failure but a success? Howe described the building's rationale: "The design is 'modern' in the sense that it is based on economic and structural logic. It is, however, subdued and dignified in ornament and coloring." This indicates a concern for both utility and decorum. Interpreting this, Jordy cited a review published just after the building was opened, in which the banking room was praised for its "simple and impressive grandeur that is unique in modern architecture." The authorship of this quality is uncertain, for it appears that while both Howe and Lescaze were very involved in the design of the interiors, an assistant named George Daub, who had worked in Vienna and with Mies van der Rohe on the Barcelona Pavilion, played a key role. Another disciple of Mies, Alfred Clauss, who had initially trained under Paul Bonatz in Stuttgart, was involved in the design of some of the furnishings and the interiors, as was a third German émigré, Walter Baermann, who had trained in Munich.[12]

Regardless of the particularities of authorship, the building's subdued dignity, laconic precision, and simplicity have been apparent to all who have tried to describe it. Did the designers seek these qualities? Were these qualities intended to be evidence of austerity, of the lean regimen the bankers and the depositors were following at the outbreak of the Great Depression? This would make the simple settings not only expressive but symbolic. Or instead, is the building's aesthetic quality the result of clear-headed thinking about practical and economic problems, as Howe the "functionalist" might have maintained?

In point of fact, Howe and Lescaze did not have this sense of functionality. On the matter of beauty, Howe approvingly cited Le Corbusier (from memory): "I am, in the final analysis, interested only in beauty." But this was neither a matter of "style" nor an aesthetic issue, if aesthetic means "disinterested," for Howe repeatedly stressed the "social" meaning of settings and buildings: "to stem the tide of our futility [that of surviving eclecticism], the functionalist has consciously declared his conviction that architecture is social, not individual, and that its ideal must conform for better or worse to the social ideal of its time."[13] Here we are, I think, directed toward an aspect of the design that contributed as much to the building's dignity as did its construction: its engagement with the city. Of all the exemplifications of the "social ideal," the city was the most durable and expressive. Many critics have noted the remarkable coordination between this building and its vicinity, a coordination that did not conform to existing motif and pattern but redefined them. The settings that resulted were not practical in the sense of quotidian; they were beyond the practical, which is to say, "ultra" practical. Howe defined architecture as "the physiognomy of culture."[14]

What is decisive in this building is the new or newly elaborated stratification of the street: from the lower landscape of the subway to the several levels of the street, to the massive body of the block, and to the upper horizon of the penthouse, solarium, observatory, and sign. Obviously, before this time buildings had basements and first floors, but never had they been elaborated in this way, never so carefully interwoven with an underground network in the first case, and as the upper horizon of streetscape in the second. Nor had the remote horizon of the city before been made such an important aspect of office interiors, which was the result of the cantilevers and "horizontality" the architects were so insistent about; the same can be said for the connections to the far distance established by the top of the building—receiving light and allowing unparalleled views from within the building and remaking the city skyline from without. The genius of the building is to integrate these strata into one section, giving to each its dimension, settings, material and luminous qualities, and "distance." In my view this is the *ultra* of "ultrapracticality" because it is where the building transcends itself as an accommodation of particular functions and becomes an urban receptacle that awaits and will accommodate patterns of behavior as yet unnamed. The building has allowed a hotel to succeed the bank because its geometry and materials are enmeshed in the primary situations and order of the urban location.

But to suggest that this sort of practicality is beyond the actual program of uses is not to say that it could be realized apart from them, as if something essential could be realized apart from something accidental. When speaking of practical matters, one might replace the metaphor of "beyond" with one of "through," which is to say that this new urban horizon or set of horizons was realized by means of the particularities of the bank. But it is, as I have tried to argue, at the same time a structure or configuration that tolerates, even invites, other particularities of use. With this in mind, one can understand its continued relevance as a part of the city and its standing as one of its exemplary forms. The PSFS Building represents the discovery of a new urban structure through the minute and exact particularities of an institution, as if that structure had existed there all along.

2001

Notes

1. The PSFS Building has been repeatedly and thoroughly studied since it was built. For historical, contextual, and biographical information, the most helpful sources are William Jordy, "PSFS: Its Development and Its Significance in Modern Architecture," *Journal of the Society of Architectural Historians,* May 1962; and again in the revised but reduced version of the same article, "The American Acceptance of the International Style," in *American Buildings and Their Architects* (Garden City, N.Y.: Doubleday, 1972); Robert Stern, "PSFS: Beaux-Arts Theory and Rational Expressionism," *Journal of the Society of Architectural Historians,* May 1962, 84–95, appendices 95–102; Robert A. M. Stern, *George Howe: Toward a Modern American Architecture* (New Haven, Conn.: Yale University Press, 1975), 108–57; Frederick Gutheim, "Saving Fund Society Building: A Re-appraisal: The Old Beauty," *Architectural Record,* October 1949, 88–95; and Lorraine Welling Lanmon, *William Lescaze Architect* (Philadelphia: Art Alliance Press; London: Associated University Presses, 1987). A comprehensive and

beautifully reproduced selection of photographs of the building, together with some drawn details of its construction, can be found in *Perspecta* 25 (1989): 138–40.

2. George Howe, "Functional Aesthetics and the Social Ideal," *Pencil Points,* April 1932, 215.

3. Le Corbusier, *The Decorative Art of Today* (London: Architectural Press, 1987), 79. Le Corbusier also criticized some settings for being too "talkative" and too "loud." By contrast, chairs that are "commendable . . . embellish life when one is least aware of them"; Paul Boulard, "Le Salon de l'art décoratif au Grand Palais," in *L'Esprit Nouveau,* 24 June 1924, n.p.

4. Gutheim, "Saving Fund Society Building."

5. Jordy, "PFSF"; Jordy "American Acceptance of the International Style," 163.

6. Aldo Rossi, *The Architecture of the City* (Cambridge, Mass.: MIT Press, 1982), 46–47, 116–19.

7. This term, and the company's praise for the "masterpiece," are available on their Web page: loewsphiladelphia@loewshotels.com.

8. Gutheim, "Saving Fund Society Building," 93; ibid., as reprinted in *Perspecta* 25, 139.

9. Gutheim, "Saving Fund Society Building"; Stern, "PFSF"; Stern, *George Howe.*

10. Jordy, "PFSF," 72.

11. Howe, "Functional Aesthetics," 215.

12. For a brief discussion of their role, see Lanmon, *William Lescaze Architect* 52, 137. These two are also mentioned by Stern in *George Howe,* 151.

13. Howe, "Functional Aesthetics," 215.

14. George Howe to Paul Weiss, June 25, 1953, in "The Architect and the Philosopher," Howe Papers, Avery Library, Columbia University.

3

Canon and Anti-Canon: On the Fall and Rise of the A + A

Timothy M. Rohan

The reputation of few buildings has fluctuated as wildly as that of Paul Rudolph's Art and Architecture Building at Yale University. Even before its completion in 1964, it had become the subject of media scrutiny and a significant presence in architecture culture. The appearance of both building and architect on the covers of the leading architectural journals of the day seemed to signal the emergence of architecture into the realm of media-driven, Warhol-style celebrity.

In the early 1960s, Rudolph was at the top of his game. As chairman of architecture since 1958, he had made Yale the premier design school of the day. Students everywhere emulated his distinctive drawing style and use of the perspective section. Even beyond the celebrity of its designer, though, and viewed purely as architecture, the A + A, because of how it challenged the orthodoxies of Modernism, seemed assured of a place within the canon. With virtuoso skill, Rudolph linked thirty-six different levels via labyrinthine passageways and bridges that sprang across vertiginous chasms. He stacked double-height drafting rooms and studios one on top of the other, then carpeted them in pulsating orange wall-to-wall and filled them with Abstract Expressionist art, Le Corbusier sketches, Beaux-Arts plaster casts, and ornament rescued from demolished Louis Sullivan buildings. Presiding over the main drafting room was a large Roman statue of Minerva. Rudolph seemed to be winking at his own camp predilections and love of the extravagant when he put an oversized, Liberace-style candelabra, similar to those in Philip Johnson's Glass House, in the elegant penthouse reserved for architectural "stars," including the Smithsons and other Brits whom he introduced to America, who flew in on Pan-Am for quick crits and lectures.

The A + A was a roller-coaster ride of a building, one intended to instruct by arousing the senses through colorful textiles and the knobby feel of Rudolph's well-known bush-hammered concrete, a surface so rough that Vincent Scully described it as "one of the most inhospitable, indeed physically dangerous ever devised by man."[1] With this one dramatic structure, then, Rudolph seemed to have provided an alternative to the gray, soulless world of the corporatized International Style—to have devised a Modernism simultaneously colorful, textured, rough, elegant, exciting, witty, slightly vulgar, and even dangerous.

Yet the glamorous voyage of this Titanic of a building would prove brief. Not long after it was occupied, hard use and overcrowding made one observer compare the interior to a shantytown; a disastrous fire in 1969 and the unsympathetic renovations that followed destroyed whatever integrity was left. By the early 1970s, less than a decade after the first students moved in, the interior of Rudolph's building was unrecognizable. For the next thirty years, the building

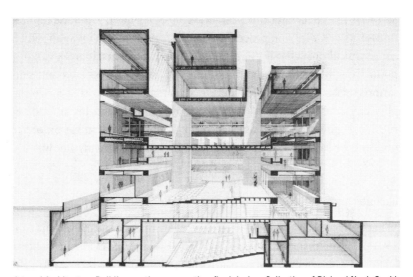

Art and Architecture Building section perspective, final design. Collection of Richard Nash Gould.

slid further and further into sad decrepitude. And this decay was mirrored by the decline of Rudolph's reputation, which fell hard with the rise of architectural Postmodernism in the late 1970s. For many, the condition of the building seemed a kind of proof of the shortcomings of Rudolph's architecture.

All this is about to change. Renovations begun in the summer of 2000 have removed many of the partitions that had darkened and divided the interiors, making it possible, for the first time in more than thirty-five years, to see the space Rudolph intended us to see. Skidmore, Owings & Merrill, under the direction of David Childs, is scheduled to complete the restoration by 2004. A 1967 alumnus of the architecture school, Childs is himself a product of the original environment of the A + A. So far, restoration efforts have dramatically revealed aspects of Rudolph's architecture that the mythology surrounding the building's demise had overshadowed, such as its relationship to the campus and city around it. And Rudolph's original plans for expansion will be fulfilled with the construction of a new building by Richard Meier, located next door, housing the library and art history department.

It has been said ad nauseam that a defining characteristic of our postmodern condition is the speeding-up of events—the intensifying acceleration of cycles of decline and renewal. These days, the careers of artists can seem as brief as those of entertainers. Even so, the rise, fall, and restoration of the A + A in a mere three decades is remarkable. So too is the effect that this dramatic trajectory has had on the reputation of its creator. The process of canon formation, the way in which consensus about what is essential is arrived at, is a fascinating vantage point from which to study a building with such a checkered and sensational past. What were the circumstances and events that made the physical state and reputation of this much-anticipated building deteriorate so quickly? What does even the preliminary restoration of the building reveal that has been forgotten or was not already known?

Decline

When I first encountered the A + A as an undergraduate in the late 1980s, it was difficult to see why anyone would have considered this battered and trash-strewn ruin to be a candidate for the canon. In those late Postmodernist times, the reputation of postwar American

Modernism was at its nadir. If you mentioned "the A + A," the response from freshman to tenured faculty was practically automatic: they hated it. In his magisterial lectures, Scully showed beautiful slides of the building in its original condition and insightfully described its downfall amid the sociopolitical crises of the late 1960s. He concluded that the A + A was part of the "tragic drama" of the 1960s and that such buildings had no place in what was now the "age of irony."[2] Evidently, this was a lesson in what *not* to do. Even so, in the late 1980s, a small cadre of students and Rudolph admirers began to champion the building and even mounted a small exhibition of original drawings from Rudolph's collection.[3] But this attention was exceptional. Beyond Yale, the A + A was derided as an example of mid-1960s establishment mentality, carelessly lumped together with corporate Modernism, the very architecture it criticized, or else seen as further evidence of Modernism in its final, most alienating and decadent stage. Although Rudolph had for the most part disappeared from contemporary discussions, his A + A had become homiletic—a handy example of the canonical other, the anti-canon.

Much of the building's poor image followed from Yale's inability to maintain the A + A (along with the rest of its campus). During the economic crises of the 1970s, Yale instituted a policy of deferred maintenance—which meant almost no maintenance—which was not lifted until the late 1980s. During this time, the interior of the A + A became a shambles—dark, overcrowded, and overused.

From the beginning, though, it was recognized that the building was poorly programmed. It has been said that with the A + A, Rudolph was in the enviable position of being his own client, but the situation was more complicated. Yale president A. Whitney Griswold—who during the 1950s had made Yale into a "museum of modern architecture" with buildings by Eero Saarinen, Gordon Bunshaft, Philip Johnson, Louis Kahn, and many more—had decided that both architecture and art should be housed together to achieve a "synthesis of the arts." So in addition to pleasing Griswold, Rudolph had to accommodate the deans of the art and the architecture schools, the chairman of art, and the art history department. In this way the design process was hampered by competing agendas. Right up until the last moment, the library was pulled in and out of the design. Eventually art history remained in its own building, but as the design progressed, Rudolph found that he had to allot square footage to the departments of city planning, graphics, and sculpture.[4]

Penthouse, with relief and candelabra. Photograph by Ezra Stoller. Copyright Ezra Stoller/Esto.

The result was that too many students and too many departments were shoehorned into too small a building. The wide-open, dramatic spaces so beautifully photographed by Ezra Stoller in 1963 were soon choked with the paraphernalia that accumulates fast with the making of art and architecture. The art students especially were dissatisfied with their constricted quarters, which were too small for the ever-increasing size of their canvases. The university administration was shocked when, in a foretaste of the campus unrest later in the decade, the artists picketed the dedication ceremonies, shot out a window with a BB gun, and covered the walls with graffiti. A building that had been conceived amid the relative cold war consensus of the second Eisenhower administration was baptized in the traumatic times that followed the Kennedy assassination.

The hoopla surrounding the dedication ceremonies in late 1963 was muted by the death of Griswold. And despite the widespread press coverage, critical reception of the building was not as uniformly positive as some remember. To Rudolph's chagrin, Nikolaus Pevsner defended old-guard Modernism with a dedication speech that warned students not to emulate the building because it was too "individualistic."[5] Although the American architectural press covered the building extensively, they peppered—and pestered—Rudolph with questions about just how well the A + A fulfilled its functional requirements. Within the school, too, there occurred a shift away from Rudolph's thinking about architecture as art and toward less formal and more socially based methods of investigation, such as those advocated by Serge Chermayeff, whom Rudolph had made a member of the faculty.[6]

His task completed, and sensing that richer opportunities lay elsewhere, Rudolph left Yale in 1965 to pursue private practice. The selection of Charles Moore to succeed Rudolph as chairman of architecture signaled what some saw as a "newly permissive" attitude, a reflection of the zeitgeist. The architecture students rebelled against the building by reconstructing Rudolph's carrels to their own specifications, even turning some of them into two-story structures. Rudolph's already worn orange carpets were replaced with earth-toned ones that darkened the palette of the interior. In a democratizing gesture, the school turned the penthouse apartment into a coffeehouse.

Rudolph and Moore had much in common, but the architecture they produced looked very different. The two architects shared their generation's interest in regionalism, the vernacular, and psychological responses to space. Both homosexual, they shared as well a camp sensibility, although this too they expressed differently. Rudolph's indulgence in camp was secretive and introverted, while Moore's was extroverted and flamboyant. And each formulated very different aesthetic responses to the asceticism of the early 1950s. For the rest of his career, Rudolph would expand on a Modernist philosophy, derived first from his training under Walter Gropius at Harvard and later expressed in a geometric vocabulary influenced by Frank Lloyd Wright and Le Corbusier; Moore's interest in regionalism, the vernacular, and historical allusion would develop into a riotous and colorful Postmodernism.

Under Moore's leadership, Yale became the setting for some of the most interesting experiments of the late 1960s Supergraphics movement—many of which were pointed critiques of Rudolph's architecture. In 1968, Moore, F. R. R. Drury, Kent Bloomer, and a group of students built a large rectangular structure whose diagonal placement in the center of the main exhibition room was intended to critique the "squareness" of the architecture. Called "Project Argus," the structure featured controlled lighting effects; within, slides and short films designed by the lighting group Pulsa were shown continuously. To some observers, though, Project Argus seemed less a refutation than an expansion of Rudolph's ideas; the critic C. Ray Smith noted that the A + A was already so visually dense and complex that the light show seemed to fulfill the promise of Rudolph's vision and to indicate the direction in which his architecture was now developing.[7]

By the late 1960s, even the mainstream architectural press that had been its supporter was criticizing the A + A. In a 1967 *Architectural Forum* article that would prove extremely damaging for Rudolph, Ellen Perry Berkeley discussed the physical decline of the building. Berkeley wrote approvingly about how the students had "spontaneously" reconfigured the interior to their own specifications by rebuilding and personalizing their carrels; they had in effect colonized the building, transforming the main drafting room into a "settlement." Berkeley said that these structures, now common to many architectural schools, resembled the favelas, or shantytowns, found on the outskirts of Latin American cities. (Period discussions about places like Brasília often saw the presence of the favela as proof of the inadequacies of Modernism.) Still, Berkeley's tone was evenhanded, and Rudolph was invited to explain his various decisions.

But the images that accompanied the article were damning. Berkeley contrasted candid photographs of the interior in its present state—which focused on the "favelas," the anti-Rudolph graffiti, and the cardboard boxes stored beneath the stairways—with the immaculate images made by Stoller in 1963. The implication was clear: the building had failed in the same way that the Establishment itself was failing, and it was left to "youth" to move in and to generate more open-ended, flexible, and spontaneous practices.[8] Indeed, both Project Argus and the favela were a critique, in built form, of the curriculum of the school itself, which the students saw as inflexible and "not relevant" to their concerns.

Rudolph blamed the article for the loss of several commissions. He was even fired from some jobs, like the Southeastern Massachusetts Technical Institute, because he was thought to be too artistic, and therefore too expensive, for large public projects. The late 1960s and early 1970s proved to be a difficult time for Rudolph, as many of his larger commissions, such as the Boston Government Services Center, which were funded by Great Society legislation, ground to a halt as the political will that had fostered them faltered.

At the same time, Rudolph became the object of yet another devastating critique, this one in Robert Venturi, Denise Scott Brown, and Steven Izenour's 1972 *Learning from Las Vegas*.[9] In the book, Rudolph's Crawford Manor Housing for the Elderly was compared to Venturi's Guild House, with Rudolph's building characterized as heroic, abstract, and high art, while Venturi's was seen as ugly, ordinary, a mix of high and low. The choice of Rudolph as the exemplar of High Modernist practices was not accidental. Yale had, in fact, been the school that sponsored the studios upon which the book was based. The A + A had functioned as an incubator for the thinking of the authors; in this way the A + A itself had become part of the internal critique of Modernism that would lead to the rise of Postmodernism. *Learning from Las Vegas* cemented Rudolph's curious position in the anti-canon; he was an essential part of this book, which would itself become part of a new, emerging canon and a fundamental text for the Postmodernist movement that would scorn him.

Although often included, Rudolph seemed unable to influence discussions and debates after 1968. Having left the lively intellectual environment of Yale, Rudolph was cut off from developments within architectural discourse. Alone in his studio, he seemed to turn inward. Unlike Philip Johnson, who easily adjusted his work and thinking to the tempo of the post-1968 period, Rudolph seemed unable to change with the times. When his camp sensibility entered into his architecture, it did so as something private, revealed only to the cognoscenti through visual clues and tricks. Rudolph seemed unable to successfully transform his ideas into a pop architecture that could become part of the new Postmodernist sensibility.

Like most campuses, Yale in the late 1960s was the scene of mass demonstrations against the war in Vietnam. The Black Panther trials were also held in New Haven—an event that might have become violent had not Yale president Kingman Brewster tempered the university's response. Because of its large spaces and abundance of materials that could be used to make signs, the architecture school became a staging ground for protests. Within the school, tensions rose when some students and faculty in the city planning department demanded that the university admit more black and Hispanic students. In June 1969, the upper two floors, the artist's studios and architectural drafting rooms, ignited and burnt under circumstances perceived as mysterious. Rumors circulated that the students themselves had set fire to the building that had come to symbolize the older generation. The truth was simpler: the fire was an accident, the result of the combustion of solvents, paint thinners, and an ever-proliferating mass of paper. The favela was as combustible as any shantytown. In a sense, the interior was immolated by its own production. Art and architecture burnt Art and Architecture. A photograph of Minerva presiding over the ruins of the drafting room was widely circulated in the press, taken as proof of the collapse of the whole enterprise. This alluring and tragic image has been regularly reprinted.[10]

The post-fire renovation was emphatically unsympathetic. Mezzanine levels and partitions were inserted, windows covered over, interior vistas blocked. The interior became significantly darker and seemed more crowded than ever. For the next thirty years, the building was a sad semiruin that fit comfortably into neither Modern nor Postmodern categories.

Renovation

Today, the ideological dust at Yale seems to be settling even as construction proceeds. Rudolph's former student and ardent admirer Robert A. M. Stern, now dean of the architecture school, has catalyzed the restoration and renovation of the A + A. Yale itself is rebuilding its campus after years of neglect. The relocation of the art students to their own building on Chapel Street—a move that should have happened thirty-five years ago—has relieved the cramped conditions. The building feels more neat and orderly than I have ever seen it, due partly to simple maintenance.

More important, the work that began a year ago has opened up vistas that were blocked for decades. Once again it is possible to look down from floor to floor along diagonal axes deep into the space, as in the views created in Rudolph's arresting drawings. In the main exhibition room, for instance, a wall has been removed, and one can see out to the street and into the library below at the same time. It is as if an etching by Piranesi had been brought to life.

The comparison of Rudolph with Piranesi is valid, for in its original incarnation Rudolph's building functioned as a kind of prephotographic viewing apparatus, a camera obscura that dramatically framed specific interior elements. Views of the city, the campus, and the users themselves were intended to inspire the student. Like those of Piranesi, these interiors were the product of a fevered and impassioned imagination whose designs could make the viewer—or inhabitant—uneasy. Rudolph's process was less a machine for producing design in a rational manner than it was an apparatus attuned to the sort of gaze that could envision an architecture based on vistas, textures, and the inchoate, half-understood signs littered throughout the building, like the Beaux-Arts plaster casts and Sullivan's ornamental panels. Rudolph's is a formal gaze, but it was unexpectedly flexible, and it inspired an architecture of emotion and action charged with the same heroic ethos as Abstract Expressionist painting. In one of his talks from the mid-1950s, Rudolph had said, "We need sequences of space which arouse one's curiosity, give a sense of anticipation, which beckon and impel us to rush forward to find that releasing space which dominates, which climaxes and acts as a magnet, and gives direction."[11] Considered in this light, the restoration of the building can be viewed as a process of cleaning out the dust and particles—the partitions and insertions—that clogged the workings of the apparatus.

Unlike those of Piranesi, Rudolph's complex interiors are outward looking. This is most evident in the main drafting room, whose interior is now flooded with light, following the removal of the partitions that had blocked the windows. In addition to brightening the interior, the exposure of the windows has made visible a whole other aspect of Rudolph's design: his commitment to urbanism. Contemporary criticism always noted that despite its bulk and size, the building was beautifully calibrated to the scale of the smaller surrounding buildings. At the A + A, and in previous projects like the Jewett Art Center at Wellesley College, Rudolph carefully inserted new buildings into existing Collegiate Gothic campuses. The dilemma his work confronted, and which would be pursued by Postmodernist experiments in urbanism, was that of context in the urban environment. It is precisely this aspect of the A + A and of Rudolph's thinking in general that has been underappreciated. Rudolph's contemporaries, like Ulrich Franzen, have agreed that the ongoing discussion of urbanism was his main contribution to the Yale school of architecture.

The removal of the interior partitions has made evident how attuned the building is to the city and the campus. The spires of Yale are now visible on all sides of the drafting room. The student looking up from the drafting board, or computer screen, once again can view the towers of Yale and New Haven on the horizon and, as a result, is perhaps encouraged to think of his or her project in a broader, more urbanistic way. Before the partitions were removed, I had thought of the main drafting room as an insular space, somewhat like the interior of Wright's Unity Temple. Now that the views to the outside have been reopened, the space seems less like an enclosed box intended to encourage concentration and more like a Japanese paper lantern suspended in an open wooden framework. The contrast between transparent and opaque is the fulfillment of Rudolph's axiom: "we need caves as well as goldfish bowls." Light pours in during the day; at night the lights within illuminate the street.

At the front of the room, a section of flooring that had been inserted to link the north and south mezzanines has been removed and replaced with a lightweight bridge. The west elevation of Louis Kahn's Yale University Art Gallery is once again visible through windows overlooking York Street. Rudolph deliberately sited the A + A so that the reflective surface of the art gallery's curtain wall captured the solid mass of his own building. With this juxtaposition, Rudolph suggests that the monotony and alienation of the modern city, lined with glass buildings like those being constructed then on Park Avenue, would be alleviated if masonry and glass were allowed to play off one another. From the corner of the building that juts forward at the intersection of Chapel and York Streets, one can again see all the way to the New Haven Green. This visual link reaffirms the connection between town and gown. In this way architecture, housed in this building that represents it, regards the city. The view recapitulates how Rudolph conceived of Chapel Street as a processional route (similar to what Johnson had described in his widely read article on the processional) that led from the green to his building.[12] Rudolph considered the A + A to be the gateway to the campus, positioned just where the colonial grid of the town ended and the modern extension of the city began.

From the rear of the top-floor studio, West Rock—one of New Haven's natural acropolises—is now more visible than ever, since a mezzanine thoughtlessly inserted has been removed. That the building is oriented to the rocks on the horizon reminds one that Rudolph had attended the lectures that became Scully's study of ritual, topography, and the Greek temple, *The Earth, the Temple, and the Gods,* and also that he had studied closely the roof of Le Corbusier's Unité d'Habitation.[13] The removal of this mezzanine has left a long horizontal mark on the wall behind; this mark should be left, like a scar, as a memento of the vicissitudes this structure has suffered.

Now that thirty years of insensitive accretions have been removed,

A + A Building with students' "favelas," circa 1967. Photograph by Roy Berkeley from Architectural Forum, July/August 1967.

the real work can begin. "The building has been burned and renovated several times," Stern told the *Yale Daily News* recently. "It's time to get it right."[14]

Rudolph always considered the building incomplete. He was, he said, aware of the overcrowded conditions and had planned for its expansion; he intended that the structure should be expanded to the north, like a megastructure. By expanding along York Street, Meier's new building will follow where Rudolph's building left off. In fact, there is already a strip of floor-to-ceiling windows along the north wall that seems like a doorway to future expansion. For Meier, the issue of context will replay itself again, as he confronts the problem of how to design a structure that will not be overpowered by the A + A. Already, Yale administrators have decreed that there will be no white porcelain enamel on the new building.

Recanonization

Rudolph himself was famously reluctant to talk about what transpired at the A + A. When I spoke to him several times before he died in 1997, he preferred to talk about new projects and other, less ill-fated buildings. Perhaps he did not need to speak about it, since the memory of the A + A was palpable. The double-height living room in his Manhattan apartment resembled the main drafting room at the A + A. In a way the entire apartment seemed like a ghostly rebuilding of the A + A penthouse in more lightweight, transparent, and illusionistic materials. In the 1980s, during the height of Postmodernism, Rudolph mostly absented himself from the American architectural scene, focusing on projects in Asia. These buildings received little attention in the Western architectural press, although articles about the decline of the A + A continued to appear. Rudolph was a ghost-like presence in architectural circles in the United States. He fell silent at a time when architects became more verbal, choosing to explain their ideas through "theory." Although articulate over the drafting board, he never successfully defended himself or verbally replied to any of the charges of his detractors. Enigmatic to the end, he has left his answers in the form of buildings.

Since Rudolph's death, and with the revival of interest in postwar Modernism within academia and popular culture, his reputation is being reassessed. Organizations have been formed and conferences held, some within the A + A, to support the cause of Modernist preservation. Rudolph is tentatively being recanonized. The A + A is part of Princeton Architectural Press's "Building Blocks," a series of pocket-size books that feature canonical buildings as photographed by Ezra Stoller. It is, however, the least popular of all the books.

2001

Notes

The author would like to thank Neil Levine and Robert A. M. Stern for their help with this article.

1. Vincent Scully, "Art and Architecture Building, Yale University," *Architectural Review*, May 1964, 332.

2. The gist of this argument is in the postscript to Vincent Scully, *Modern Architecture: The Architecture of Democracy*, rev. ed. (New York: George Braziller, 1974), 49–50.

3. See George Ranalli, *Paul Rudolph: Drawings for the Art and Architecture Building at Yale, 1959–1963* (New Haven, Conn.: Yale School of Architecture, 1988).

4. For a detailed history of the planning of the building, see Richard Pommer, "The Art and Architecture Building at Yale, Once Again," *Burlington Magazine,* December 1972, 853–61.

5. Nikolaus Pevsner, "Address Given at the Opening of the Yale School of Art and Architecture, 1963," *Studies in Art, Architecture, and Design,* vol. 2 (New York: Walker, 1968), 260–65.

6. For a detailed analysis of the politics of the Yale School, see Robert A. M. Stern, "Yale 1950–1960," *Oppositions* 4 (October 1974): 35–62.

7. C. Ray Smith, *Supermannerism: New Attitudes in Post-Modern Architecture* (New York: E. P. Dutton, 1977), 108–10.

8. Ellen Perry Berkeley, "Architecture on the Campus: Yale: A Building as a Teacher," *Architectural Forum,* July/August 1967, 47–53.

9. Robert Venturi, Denise Scott Brown, and Steven Izenour, *Learning from Las Vegas* (Cambridge, Mass.: MIT Press, 1972).

10. The atmosphere of suspicion is captured in a news article by Joseph Lelyveld, "After Fire, Yale Smolders," *New York Times,* June 27, 1969, 39, 74. "Into the Fire," in *Perspecta* 29 (1998), provides documents about activism in the architecture school at Yale and photographs of the building after the fire. An unpublished interview that C. Ray Smith conducted on October 11, 1979, with New Haven Fire Marshall Thomas Lyden, who investigated the incident in 1969, has convinced me that the fire was an accident. The interview is part of Rudolph's papers; unprocessed documents, Paul Rudolph Archives, the Library of Congress.

11. Paul Rudolph, "The Changing Philosophy of Architecture," *Architectural Forum,* July 1954, 120.

12. Philip Johnson, "Whence and Whither: The Processional Element in Architecture," *Perspecta* 9/10 (1965): 17–56.

13. Vincent Scully, *The Earth, the Temple, and the Gods: Greek Sacred Architecture* (New Haven, Conn.: Yale University Press, 1962).

14. Chris Rovzar, "Top Architects Hired to Design Art Area Projects," *Yale Daily News,* February 5, 2001, 3.

4

Canons in Cross Fire: On the Importance of Critical Modernism

Charles Jencks

The idea that there is a canon of Modern architecture is, paradoxically, insisted upon by people who know perfectly well that there is no such thing. Neutral, abstract, and in some variant of the International Style, this great white canon causes mental snow blindness, convincing people that a single Modernism exists—at the same time as they dismiss the idea as absurd. This contradiction, entrenched in the architectural landscape, opens up important issues, but before pursuing them, let us consider other fields where canons carry a bigger charge, for instance, religion, literature, and Modern art.

For the Pope there are the canonic scriptures and doctrines that define Catholicism, and it falls to the Vatican's Congregation for the Doctrine of the Faith and its prefect, Cardinal Ratzinger, to define those canons. Successor to the Inquisition, this Congregation effectively shores up orthodoxy and expels those who deviate from the doctrinal line, such as the creative Catholics Matthew Fox and Hans Kung. For F. R. Leavis, and many literary critics, there was a canonic Great Tradition of literature that always needed asserting, upholding, and reevaluating by those of supposedly superior sensibility.[1] Harold Bloom recently has defined a broader set of great works in his defense of an embattled tradition, and he has given it a suitably definitive appellation, *The Western Canon*.[2]

For Alfred H. Barr and the founders of the Museum of Modern Art, the canonic story of Modern art led from Neo-Impressionism through Fauvism to Cubism, the Bauhaus and Modern Architecture (capitalized, as the gospel ought to be). This canonic trajectory led directly to Abstract Art, and it determined the arrangement of works in the galleries of MoMA right into the 1980s. This canon also justified a view of history as aiming toward abstraction as its goal and, at the same time, validated the major bloodline of Modern artists from Picasso through Jackson Pollock, a lineage sanctioned in the critical writings of Clement Greenberg. This orthodoxy lasted until just last year, when the refurbishment of MoMA—and of course of Postmodernism too—forced an entire reevaluation of the collection, at which point a messy and interesting set of plural categories led to a reconceptualization of the history of Modern art. The new groupings, categorized by subject rather than historical period, varied in cogency, as did the similar new arrangement at the Tate Modern in London. (This shift in canons is, of course, only a provisional attempt to contend with the challenge of pluralism. One looks forward to the next, and more considered, synthesis.)

For Sigfried Giedion, as I was taught at Harvard in the 1960s, there was a "New Tradition" of Modern architects that needed defending and promoting (subtracted of Expressionists and others who did not fit within the canon according to CIAM). For Bruno Zevi, there was a similar great tradition, but it culminated in the very architects Giedion had dismissed as "transitory facts." And so it went, and so it goes. When I was a young historian studying under Reyner Banham, I wrote a paper, "History as Myth," which showed how each successive historian rewrote the script of Modernism by putting back into the story some of what the previous critic had excised, only to perpetuate a new bias of his own. Banham was no exception to the rule, as he enjoyed pointing out, and when once questioned on this process of historians' one-upmanship and asked how to explain it, he said, "apostolic succession." Modern architectural historians, like defenders of the True Faith, were people of the book; they passed on beliefs by studying and worshipping in the same church.

The delicious irony of this situation was inescapable, for the tradition being canonized was purportedly based on revolution; one has to remember hard what Modernism once claimed to be: avant-garde, revolutionary, new, idealistic, utopian. The idea of being radical and progressive and shocking carried Modernism throughout the nineteenth century and up to the 1930s. How, I once asked Philip Johnson, could the Museum of *Modern* Art be both a museum *and* radical, both "the American canonization of something that had been done," the Establishment, *and* adversarial? "Easy," he answered with stunning pragmatic nonchalance, "It succeeded. . . . You can still have the paradox and fortunately go on designing anyway you like." Canons are there to be affirmed and broken according to a logic no one understands. Modernism means both the triumph of corporate conformity and its constant overthrow, an idea I would christen "Johnson's Confusion," since he pointed it out so clearly.[3]

Direct contradictions are no harder for the High Church of Modernism than they are for the Vatican. In fact, both thrive on them. We are back at the paradox with which I started, but before addressing it directly, I want to rehearse the architecture of the past century and, with the aid of a diagram, put forward the proposition that there is also a tradition that bubbles away under the surface: Critical Modernism. Whereas canonic Modernism today dominates the academies and institutes of architecture, as well as the architecture of big-city downtowns, Critical Modernism is a creative avant-garde always reloading its canons in response to a perceived imbalance and, of course, a creative opportunity.

Glance at the evolutionary tree of the twentieth century that I have constructed around six underlying traditions.[4] Clearly, the main narrative does not belong to any building type, movement, or individual. It quickly dismisses any idea of a single canon—white, machine aesthetic, abstract, or minimalist. Rather, it displays a competitive drama, a dynamic and turbulent flow of ideas, social movements, technical forces, and individuals, all jockeying for position. A movement or an individual may be momentarily in the public eye and enjoy media power, but such notoriety rarely lasts more than five years and usually not more than two. It is true that certain architects of the previous century—how strange those words ring for Old Modernists—exerted creative forces that lasted far longer. Ludwig Mies van der Rohe was a power to reckon with in the 1920s and 1960s. Le Corbusier, Frank Lloyd Wright, and Alvar Aalto, who with Mies made up the big four, were seminal for decades. And Louis Kahn, James Stirling, Norman Foster, Peter Eisenman, Frank Gehry, and Rem Koolhaas, the little six, each had two small periods of influence. But these protean characters, to stay relevant and on top, also had to reinvent themselves every ten years or so.

The notion that there is a "ten-year rule" of reinvention for the creative genius in the twentieth century has been well argued by the Harvard cognitive scientist Howard Gardner. In *Creating Minds: An Anatomy of Creativity Seen through the Lives of Freud, Einstein, Picasso, Stravinsky, Eliot, Graham, and Gandhi,* Gardner studies these major Modernists, showing how they made breakthroughs or creatively shifted their thinking every ten years.[5] In a recent book, *Le Corbusier and the Continual Revolution in Architecture,* I have found the same pattern in this the Proteus of design. As the Hayward Gallery put it, polemically, in the title of a 1987 retrospective, Le Corbusier was the "Architect of the Century."[6] Well, could this be possible—even before the century was over and Frank Gehry was given a shot at the title? I think the answer is "yes," as I argue at length and as the diagram shows. Le Corbusier appears on this chart at five points: as the seminal designer of the "Heroic Period" of the 1920s, as a forceful thinker of a new (and rather unfortunate) urbanism, as the leader of CIAM and the movement to design mass housing after the war, as a harbinger of Postmodernism with the church at Ronchamp and the symbolic architecture of Chandigarh, and, at the end of his life, as a forerunner of High-Tech, with his pavilions in Brussels and Zurich. No other architect was so creative in so many different traditions. Not for nothing was he seen as "the Picasso of architecture," and importantly for my argument, the seminal buildings of each of his creative periods expressed different canons. (Many critics and architects, including Nikolaus Pevsner and James Stirling, were upset when Ronchamp, with its primitive expression, seemed to deny Le Corbusier's devotion to the Machine Aesthetic.) There was no single "Modern Architecture" to which he was faithful—only, perhaps, the basic principle of being critical and creative.

But the point of my argument is slightly different from Gardner's. While agreeing with his analysis, I think that one of the important reasons for the demonic creativity of his seven "geniuses" is that the past century was uncommonly turbulent. My diagram, with its tortuous blobs, is meant to capture this condition of continual revolution. At any one time, the twentieth-century architect has had to face three or four competing movements of architecture and respond to broad changes in technology, social forces, style, and ideology—not to mention world wars and such large impersonal realities as the rise of the Internet and digital media. It was an exhausting century. As the Chinese proverb puts it: May you be cursed to live in interesting

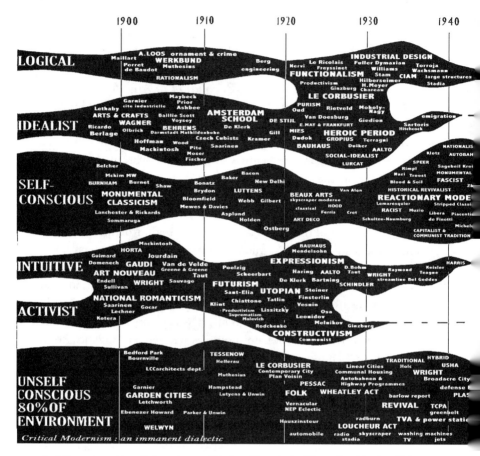

Evolutionary tree of twentieth-century architecture: Six major traditions of architecture (listed, far left) oscillate with respect to each other, like species. About sixty explicit movements or schools emerged in the twentieth century, as did one hundred social trends, technologies, and building types. In general, the evaluation of the significance of any architect (four hundred are included here) is based on consensus, although some judgments are arguable (such as the supreme importance of Gaudí); historians and critics who have shaped opinion or theory are also noted here. The competitive pluralism that this diagram shows—four to five movements at any one time and a new movement or trend every five years—has been the engine of continual revolution. The dominant self-conscious tradition, first classical and then corporate Modern, successfully suppressed the power though not the influence of other traditions. Expressionist schools and participatory design were born several times, never to become the

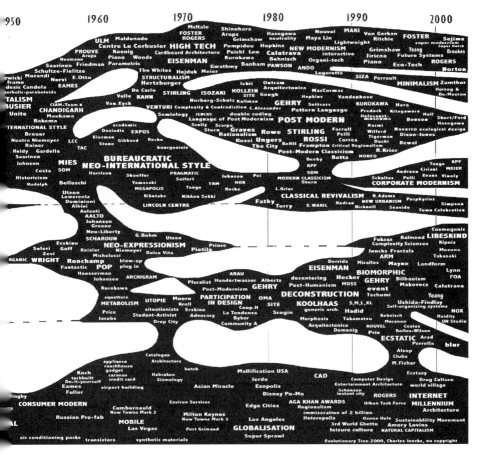

The diagram shows a timeline with years: 1950, 1960, 1970, 1980, 1990, 2000.

mainstream. Postmodernism, for a short time in the late 1970s and early 1980s, challenged its supremacy but then became commercialized. Today the Biomorphic School is a creative alternative to mainstream Modernism, but it has yet to develop either the strength or following of its competitors, suggesting a truth revealed by the diagram: it shows creative, conscious movements rather than quantities of buildings.

This diagram should be in three dimensions to be able to show how all traditions relate simultaneously. The two dimensions create two kinds of anomalies. For instance, Eisenman and Cardboard Architecture are next to Foster, Rogers, and High-Tech in 1973 because these different approaches are variants of the Logical tradition. Second, some architects, such as Mackintosh and Le Corbusier, are in more than one tradition because they move around or cut across many categories. All diagrams produce some distortions. (By Charles Jencks, 2000) times. To keep at the top of the profession, or at least stay influential, an architect has had to revolutionize his ideas about every ten years. In other words, the impetus for creativity comes from without as much as from within.

But no matter how beneficent this perpetual upheaval and reinvention may have been for architecture, it has not been good for the environment. For one thing, the ideas being constantly reinvented have been *his* ideas—*men* have dominated the revolutionary period; among the four hundred protean creators gathered in my diagram, there are few women. An urbanism both more feminine and also more coherent would have been far superior to the characteristically masculine, over-rationalized, and badly related boxes that have marred our cities. For another thing, continual revolution, or the constant change of fashion, business cycles, technical innovations, and social transformations, has meant that most architecture, like most production in the other arts, has lacked the depth and perfection possible in earlier centuries. It is hard to master an art while surfing the waves of "what's next." Nonetheless, that is what the past century has been, a constant motion of whirls and eddies. My diagram shows about a hundred trends and technical forces, and sixty movements, many of them "isms"—like Futurism, Purism, Expressionism, Brutalism, and Metabolism—that became "was-isms." Riding these waves as a leader is exhilarating, until inevitably the neo-follower surfs on by.

I do not mean to be disparaging so much as realistic. The twentieth century produced great architecture but, as Lewis Mumford often noted, great architecture that had great faults. A Critical Modernism acknowledges these problems, faces the horrors as much as the triumphs, and responds to them dialectically. Critical Modernism is Modernism critical of itself.

When historians look at the past, they typically do so with eyes carefully focused on a few canons, and these conceptual glasses can rigidly exclude the variety, contradictions, mess, and creative wealth of a period. Furthermore, as readers we often appreciate and applaud them for their myopia. All history writing is selective, and while there is no way around this, I have devised the evolutionary tree precisely to compensate for the perspectival distortions. If not wholly inclusive, it is, at least, balanced in its selective effects. As can be seen in the classifiers on the far left of the diagram, the tree is based on the assumption that there are coherent traditions that tend to self-organize around underlying structures. Often opposed to each other psychologically and culturally, these deep structures act like what are called, in the esoteric science of nonlinear dynamics, "attractor basins." They attract architects to one line of development rather than to another. Why? Not only because of taste, training, education, and friendships but also because of typecasting and of how the market encourages—almost forces—architects to have an identifiable style and skill—in a word, to specialize.

Of course, architects dislike being pigeonholed as much as do politicians and writers—they too like to claim universality, freedom, and openness. But it is the rare architect, such as Le Corbusier or Gehry, who can be found in different traditions, and often such an architect is pilloried for abandoning one set of canonical beliefs for another. Enough forces conspire to keep architects "on message," even when they seek, like Postmodernists, to be pluralists.

Surprises

What tales does this turbulent blob-diagram tell? In crude terms, it reveals several unlikely points. Most architecture—80 percent?—is by non-architects, or at least is the result of larger processes that are, artistically speaking, "unself-conscious": building regulations, governmental acts, the vernacular tradition, planning laws, mass housing, the malling of the suburbs, and inventions in the technical/industrial sphere. Le Corbusier in the 1920s, Russian disurbanists in the 1930s, and Richard Rogers today (working with Tony Blair) try to affect this inchoate area, but it is, like globalization, mostly beyond anyone's control. This high proportion of nonarchitectural creativity is likely to lessen in the future as more and more of the environment is guided by governmental and planning control, responding to economic and ecological forces. But the ironic truth remains that in terms of control and megaplanning, the Disney Corporation has been more effective than the former Soviet Union; of course, architecturally speaking, its results have been unself-conscious vernacular pastiche, all too consciously applied.

Another surprise emerging from the diagram is that a polemical movement may not be the preserve of just one tradition. One would have thought the ecological imperative might have been monopolized by the Activist tradition, but it has been taken up by all the traditions in different ways. For instance, the classicists, following Leon Krier, have created an ecological movement they have christened with the contentious brand "New Urbanism." New Urbanism is based on the tight village planning of a previous era, and its green credentials are presented with historicist wrappers. Then there are Postmodern versions of green architecture, including work by SITE, Ralph Erskine, and Lucien Kroll; high-tech versions usually called Eco-Tech (or Organi-Tech); and the Biomorphic versions of the Malaysian Ken Yeang. And there is the madly optimistic corporate-governmental version of the Sustainability Movement led by Amory Lovins. His notion is summarized in the oxymoron "Natural Capitalism," which suggests that nature and capitalism can walk hand in hand in the twenty-first century.[7] My point is that, counter to intuition and previous issue-based movements, green architecture comes in all styles and traditions.

A third surprise is that we can see strange alliances within the self-conscious tradition, usually the mainstream, or what Sigfried Giedion damned as the "ruling style" of architecture. Through the 1940s, this style was mostly a version of classicism: Edwardian Baroque, Beaux-Arts Classicism, monumental stripped classicism, or the fundamental classicism of Gunnar Asplund. When the Fascists in Italy and Spain and the leaders of Nazi Germany and Stalinist Russia imposed their versions of classicism as a state style, contending approaches were quashed. The diaspora of Modern architects and the waning of other approaches are clear from the diagram. Like evolutionary species whose habitat is destroyed, the Modernists became virtually extinct—or else they emigrated from Europe and the USSR.

Influenced by social geographers such as David Harvey and Jeffrey Herf, I have called these classical or monumental folk architects "Reactionary Modernists."[8] Like Albert Speer, they were just as wedded to technology, economic progress, instrumental reason, and the zeitgeist as Mies, Le Corbusier, and Gropius. The fact that they persecuted functionalists and creative Modernists, and adopted reactionary styles and attitudes, has obscured the deeper point that they shared the Modernists' assumptions about power, mass culture, and mass production. They all were, in effect, disputing some common territory, a point that the diagram reveals, especially when Modernism triumphs after the Second World War.

The true inheritors of the postwar mainstream were the big corporate Modernists, and they have been so ever since. They appear small in my diagram because their creativity has not been that significant. In terms of volume of work, however, they have greatly overshadowed the four other conscious traditions. This begins to explain the paradox with which I started. Modernism does indeed exist as the mainstream, a corporate one, but the more creative movements that contest it are critical of this dominance and the harm it does to the environment. Too often and easily, we term both the larger corporate Modernism *and* the reactions to it "Modernist," without much reflection on the glaring contradiction inherent in this confusion.

The evolutionary tree also shows how the mainstream is constantly attracted back to stripped classicism or degree-zero Modernism. Although they are all very different, Lincoln Center in New York and twenty other cultural centers in America during the 1960s are in this bloodline, as is the Modern Classicism of Robert A. M. Stern and Demetri Porphyrios. The corporate Modernism of Renzo Piano in Berlin, and even Richard Meier at the Getty, is not too far away from this "strange attractor." Why? The institutional forces of production and patronage favor an impersonal, abstract, semiclassical sobriety. In Giedion's view, the "ruling taste" is usually pulled toward this attractor basin, even if today the idea might have given him pause for thought.

But this tendency of the "ruling taste" toward self-conscious traditionalism and now corporate Modernism is inherent in Critical Modernism, which always reacts against the dominant. Consider Le Corbusier himself in the 1960s, at the height of his fame, when he was bitterly fighting the destruction of Paris by grandiose Modernist projects, such as Bernard Zehrfuss's big dumb dome in La Defense. Or, as he fulminated somewhat earlier, "In 1956 L-C was asked to accept membership of the Institut de France (Academie des Beaux Arts) in Paris: 'Thank you, never!' . . . My name would serve as a banner to conceal the present evolution of the Ecole des Beaux Arts towards a superficial modernism."[9] Le Corbusier's outburst is a good example of what I mean by Critical Modernism as a constant, underground contradictory force, but, unfortunately, his example was not heeded, and "superficial modernism" has been dominant ever since.

Yet mainstream culture is not always located on this axis. Several important exceptions occurred when Expressionism, the Bauhaus, and the Heroic Period dominated for a few years in the 1920s, and when Postmodernism did in the early 1980s, and Art Nouveau and National Romanticism did at the start of the century. Hector Guimard in Paris, Victor Horta in Belgium, Charles Rennie Mackintosh in Glasgow, Eliel Saarinen and Lars Sonck in Helsinki, Otto Wagner in

Vienna, and my favorite architect, Antonio Gaudí, in Barcelona—all became momentary leaders of a major public architecture, if only for a few years and in a few cities.

Gaudí

My bias shows through the evolutionary tree at one point. Nikolaus Pevsner dismissed most of the movements cited just above as "transitory fashions," and for Sigfried Giedion, except for the Heroic Period, they were not "constituent facts." One remembers how Modernist historians, like revisionist apparatchiks airbrushing Trotsky out of photographs, liked to clean up uncomfortable facts. Interpretation and judgment distort all historical selection. My argument for placing Antonio Gaudí as *the* architect of the century, on a par with Le Corbusier, does not rest on his influence, city planning, or theoretical contribution. Rather, it rests on his creative brilliance in turning city building and structure into a high art. No other architect managed to get craftsmen, artists, and even patrons working together on such a large and complete scale. His works remain the standard for the integration of all the arts at the highest creative and symbolic level.

Antonio Gaudí, Casa Batllo, Barcelona. Doors within doors—suggestions of the human figure as well as the animal kingdom impressed on the main transition to the home. Gaudí would take functional problems (how to get large and small elements through the front door) and seek new forms and solutions. Photograph by Melba Levick.

The reason his work has such creative depth is that he took a long time—the kind of time that few twentieth-century architects would allow themselves—to innovate at all levels. Depth requires time, and since in the marketplace, time is money, depth is in short supply. Gaudí's architecture exploits all sorts of new structural types—such as the hyperbolic paraboloid—if not for the very first time, then for the first time in a seminal way. He makes diverse form types his own by giving them forceful and poetic expression. Moreover, he bends structural rationalism to expressive ends. For instance, while the Italian engineer Pier Luigi Nervi makes an ordered art from showing the isostatic lines of force in his concrete ceilings—for instance, in the Palazzo del Lavoro in Turin—Gaudí takes the same forces and expresses them dynamically, pushing against each other, like the straining muscles of an athlete. Concrete becomes animated, humorous, related to our body and moods. Beyond this, in buildings such as the Casa Batllo, he uses technological and structural innovations for symbolic and political ends—to present the sufferings of the Catalans under the dragon of Castile. His structural and material inventions are always means to a larger intention, and it is this overall meaning that gives Gaudí's work enormous symbolic depth. It communicates up and down the scales, from the everyday and local to the cosmic. By comparison, the work of Mies and Aalto seems to me too abstract, that of Le Corbusier and Wright too cut off from the language of the street, that of Eisenman too cerebral, that of Gehry too formalist.

To argue that Gaudí was the canonic architect of the century, however, reveals my partiality toward artistic and symbolic architecture, values that other critics, such as Kenneth Frampton, do not necessarily share. In an Art Net lecture of 1974, I was shocked to hear this historian dismiss Gaudí's work as kitsch—but then Philip Johnson used to dismiss Frank Lloyd Wright as the "greatest architect of the nineteenth century." The evolutionary tree is meant to make such dismissals—ones that Pevsner, Giedion, Frampton, and Johnson are happy to commit—more difficult, or at least uncomfortable. Canons contest other canons, and Critical Modernism is the dialectical response of one set of beliefs toward another that has become too stereotyped, too powerful. In this sense, like Late Modernism and Postmodernism, Critical Modernism is simply Modernism critical of its own excesses.

I realize, however, that the high placement of Gaudí is a contentious claim that needs much more defense than I can offer here.

Those who value the perfecting of architectural technique might proffer Mies, Kahn, or Norman Foster as canonic architects of the century. Those who value theory and education might favor Gropius at the Bauhaus or Eisenman because of his design and writing; those who prefer an understated humanism might put Aalto in this role. And what about contenders for "the little six," what about Lutyens, Asplund, Fuller, Niemeyer, Rogers, and Piano—or another set? Many contenders for the top positions are apparent in the weighting I have given the four hundred "best" architects, and they each presume different canons.

Let me reiterate the main speculation, or hypothesis—Critical Modernism is radically dispersed throughout the many Modern movements that exist and react to each other and to the outside world. It is distributed in many places and exists in many architects, if for only a short time, for Critical Modernism is a process of learning through absorbing and criticizing other Modernists. Moreover, what matters most is the pattern of these positions taken successively and the space of creativity they open up. One can say that the wisdom of architecture always outstrips that of any single architect and that there is a beautiful, if messy, pattern to this history that my diagram seeks to reveal. Yes, history *is*, as Winston Churchill said, "just one crazy thing after another"—it is like a drunk wandering aimlessly. But occasionally the drunk learns something and makes progress, just as the proto-Modern Movement of the nineteenth century had hoped. The problem comes when we confuse the mainstream with the critical, the white abstract style with the creative dialectic, just because they both have good claims on the word *Modern*. Those claims are socially and historically embedded, and deeply entrenched. They will not go away, so one can predict that Johnson's Confusion, and ours, will extend into the future. But that is no reason to turn it into a theory of history and fail to discriminate, especially since a canon must aim well.

2001

Notes

Those who have offered me helpful suggestions for this paper include Dennis Sharp, Peter Davey, Ivor Richards, and Geoffrey Broadbent.

1. See, for instance, F. R. Leavis, *The Great Tradition: George Eliot, Henry James, Joseph Conrad* (London: Chatto & Windus, 1948).

2. Harold Bloom, *The Western Canon: The Books and School of the Ages* (New York: Harcourt Brace, 1994).

3. "History as Myth" appears in Charles Jencks and George Baird, eds., *Meaning in Architecture* (London: Barrie & Rockliff, 1969); and "Dialogues with Philip Johnson" in *The New Moderns: From Late to Neo-Modernism,* by Charles Jencks (London: Academy Editions, 1990).

4. The evolutionary tree is further described in my *Le Corbusier: The Continual Revolution in Architecture* (New York: Monacelli Press, 2001).

5. Howard Gardner, *Creating Minds: An Anatomy of Creativity Seen through the Lives of Freud, Einstein, Picasso, Stravinsky, Eliot, Graham, and Gandhi* (New York: Basic Books, 1993).

6. The Hayward's retrospective is published in *Le Corbusier, Architect of the Century* (London: Arts Council of Great Britain, 1987).

7. Countering stereotypes, Lovins argues that with enough efficiency, economic development and ecological growth can occur at the same time—and at four times their current rate! Natural Capitalism or wishful thinking? It is no surprise that former U.S. president Bill Clinton and various business leaders have applauded Lovins's message. The trick, Lovins points out, is that we have to rethink all systems from the start. But as Oscar Wilde put it: "Being natural is such a very difficult pose to keep up." Reconciling these opposed forces will take more than a pose; it will take a raft of tax incentives and other changes that the new president George W. Bush is unlikely to accept.

8. See, for instance, Jeffrey Herf, *Reactionary Modernism: Technology, Culture, and Politics in Weimar and the Third Reich* (Cambridge: Cambridge University Press, 1984).

9. Le Corbusier, *My Work*, trans. James Palmes, introduction by Maurice Jardot (London: Architectural Press, 1960), 49–52.

5

In the Shadow of a Giant: On the Consequences of Canonization

Daniel Willis

Fame and celebrity are, ultimately, techniques of abstraction. In societies grown complex, they work to focus attention, and, like all abstractions, they simplify complicated circumstances, allowing us to deal only with who or what "matters." The mechanisms of public and professional acclaim must necessarily discriminate. In a field such as architecture, there is not enough "media space" for all practitioners to be fairly represented. Since there is no governing body of independent critics—critics untainted by the need to sell magazines, to make academic reputations, or to market their own professional work—assigned to assess the output of each architect, the apportionment of fame is never fair. However, even when the works receiving attention are deserving, as is usually the case with architectural reputations sustained over a century or more, our focus on some must necessarily cause us to ignore others. This seems to me one of the most dubious aspects of the architectural canon: not that the canon might contain undeserving works (of course it does), but that in shining so bright a light on a few buildings or projects, others are unjustly eclipsed.

This is a drawback common to all the abstracting instruments we architects employ. Not only do we have no way of knowing whether our discriminating choices have been the right ones, the very act of discriminating, of including or excluding, exaggerates differences. The canon distorts the field of architectural production much as the evening news sensationalizes the day's events. Thus, my purpose here is not so much to debate the merits of a canonized work but to examine such a work in order to see what its exalted status has revealed and—more important—concealed. The question to be considered is this: what are the effects of the "overshadowing" that occurs when an architectural work is caught in the glare of media attention, professional praise, and historical commendation? To answer it, I have chosen to study the impact of a celebrated building by an architect who cast—literally and figuratively—one of the largest shadows ever to fall on the professional landscape.

Toward the end of the nineteenth century, no architect basked in the glow of adulation more completely than did Henry Hobson Richardson (1838–86). According to architectural historian and Richardson biographer James F. O'Gorman: "[In 1885] he bestrode his profession as its most colorful and influential member. . . . During the spring of this year his colleagues nationwide picked what they thought were the ten best buildings in the country. Works by Richardson took up half the list, published in June, and his Trinity Church, on Copley Square in Boston headed the lot."[1] After his relatively short life had ended, Richardson—whose popularity with colleagues and clients owed nearly as much to his winning personality as to his talent—suffered no loss of ranking. Indeed, Richardson was one of the few nineteenth-century American architects able to maintain high standing after the rise of the Modern Movement.[2]

If Richardson was unchallenged in his day as America's most respected architect, his opinion of the greatest among his works was similarly decisive: "If they honor me for the pygmy things I have already done," he asked, "what will they say when they see Pittsburgh finished?"[3] Richardson was referring to his designs for the Allegheny County Courthouse and Jail, two related buildings that were to be built on adjacent sites in what would eventually become the government district of the city. Richardson had won the commission for these buildings (in February 1884) in a competition among five invited architects.[4] His contemporary and first biographer, Mariana Griswold Van Rensselaer, noted that Richardson suspected he was destined for a short life and "was almost feverishly anxious to see the Courthouse complete before he died."[5] She reported that Richardson considered the Courthouse "as the full expression of his mature power in the direction where it was most at home."[6]

H. H. Richardson, Allegheny County Courthouse and Jail, circa 1980. The City-County Building is visible at far right. Photograph by Clyde Hare.

It was not just the scale of the Courthouse and Jail commission that caused Richardson to believe it dwarfed his previous accomplishments. Indeed, his Marshall Field Store in Chicago would be more massive, his Trinity Church perhaps more prominent in its surroundings, and his Cincinnati Chamber of Commerce and Albany Capital buildings nearly as monumental. What the Allegheny County buildings offered was a chance for this architect, at the peak of his fame and creative powers, to pursue the design of a programmatically complex landmark building in a city Richardson was just beginning to view as a fertile market for his services.[7] The opportunity to celebrate and facilitate the cause of justice on a desirable site (the crest of what was then known as Grant's Hill) in a booming industrial metropolis must have been viewed by the ailing forty-six-year-old Richardson as one of the few remaining challenges worthy of his talents.

For the most part, historians and critics over the past 115 years have not disagreed. Boston's photogenic Trinity Church may more readily appear in historical surveys,[8] and the demolished Marshall Field Store may have been more useful to those, such as Henry-Russell Hitchcock, who wished to portray Richardson as a proto-Modernist, but no critic of whom I am aware has debated Richardson's assessment head-on. The Jail, in particular, has been extolled by architectural observers for its bold massing, lack of ornament, and extraordinary materiality. Hitchcock called the granite wall surrounding the jail "one of the most magnificent displays of fine material in the world";[9] and he reflected what would become the majority opinion when he wrote "the jail is more successful than the courthouse" (although he added "of course, [it was] a much simpler thing for Richardson to design"). Most renderings of the two buildings produced by Richardson's office, in which the Jail is nearly obscured by the Courthouse, suggest that Richardson thought otherwise, as did Van Rensselaer, who expressed the view that the Courthouse was "the most magnificent and imposing" of Richardson's works. From the description he supplied with his competition drawings, we can see that Richardson was particularly proud of the manner in which he had distributed the courtrooms and their support spaces throughout the building, and of the way natural light was admitted into the courtrooms from two sides.[10] His ingenious (if somewhat exaggerated) justification for the building's enormous tower was equally innovative: it was to provide a fresh air intake high above Pittsburgh's polluted streets.[11]

Whichever of the two buildings one considers superior, it cannot be disputed that together they were very quickly granted canonical status by professionals and interested observers alike. The critic Montgomery Schuyler, writing in 1911, placed them "among the chief ornaments of any American city."[12] Of course, the rapid assimilation of these buildings into the canon, and the position they have attained alongside a few of others regarded as Richardson's best works owe partly to the tragic circumstances of their realization. Despite Richardson's "feverish" desire to see them concluded, his death (attributed to Bright's disease) occurred when only the Jail was near completion. It would be another two years until its companion was ready for occupancy, and it was Richardson's successor firm, Shepley, Rutan and Coolidge, that oversaw the completion and furnishing of the Courthouse.

Evidence that the buildings were considered extraordinary even before they were finished can be found in contemporary coverage by the Pittsburgh news media. For example, as the nearly completed Courthouse tower was attaining its full 318 feet of height, a local newspaper observed: "The beauty and dignity of the great building dwarfing all other structures in its vicinity cannot fail to arouse a desire for better things in architecture. The new Court House silently but eloquently exerts a potent influence. As a court of justice it tells of

H. H. Richardson, Allegheny County Courthouse and Jail, circa 1980, main stairwell. Photograph by Clyde Hare.

the majesty of the law; as a thing of rare beauty in granite it preaches the gospel of better architecture in the Iron City."[13] That even the industrial barons who held the reins of Pittsburgh's sooty economy recognized Richardson's achievement can be confirmed by examining the resolution adopted by the Allegheny County commissioners, little more than a month before the Courthouse was dedicated. Noting the many requests from the architect's "friends and admirers" in Allegheny County for a suitable tribute, the commissioners resolved to place the following inscription in the building's great stairway: "In memory of Henry Hobson Richardson, Architect, 1838–1886— Genius and training made him master of his profession. Although he died in the prime of life, he left to his country many monuments of art, foremost among them this temple of justice."[14]

Having compiled this brief account of the circumstances surrounding the elevated reputations of both Richardson and the Courthouse and Jail, I can return to the question that is my main interest: What have been the consequences of this canonization? What, for example, has resulted from the "masterpiece" designation bestowed upon these buildings? What have such judgments meant to the buildings themselves, the city they occupy, and to our present-day architectural awareness?

One of the most important consequences of the canonization of the Courthouse and Jail has been the unwarranted overshadowing of another excellent building. The exuberant monumentality of Richardson's two structures, coupled with the fame of their architect, has blinded most observers to the existence of an equally remarkable structure that is their neighbor. The Pittsburgh building that today offers the most relevant lessons in civic architecture is neither the Courthouse nor the Jail but an historically obscure edifice standing approximately eighty-five feet south of them. This structure, little known outside Pittsburgh and scarcely appreciated within it, is the City-County Building, credited to the Pittsburgh architect Edward B. Lee in association with the New York firm Palmer, Hornbostel & Jones. On January 20, 1914, it was announced that Lee's team had bested fifteen others in a competition judged by architects Paul Cret of Philadelphia, John Donaldson of New York, and Burt Fenner of Detroit.[15] Construction on the building began in July 1915, and by December 1917 the mayor was able to move into his suite. It took an additional year for the building to be fully furnished and occupied. The structure provided the city and county governments with about 500,000 square feet of office space, and it cost slightly less than $2.8 million (unfurnished).

Edward Lee (1876–1956) was a Harvard-educated Pittsburgh architect who frequently worked in association with other firms. It is assumed that his role in the design of the City-County Building was secondary to that of Henry Hornbostel (1867–1961).[16] Among the circumstantial evidence supporting this conclusion is the Hartford Municipal Building (ca. 1912). This commission, also awarded through a competition, teamed Hornbostel's firm with Hartford architects-of-record Davis & Brooks. While the exterior of the building has little resemblance to anything by Hornbostel, the interior contains a dominating central circulation space similar to that of the Pittsburgh building.[17] Hornbostel's designs for several campus buildings at the Carnegie Institute of Technology (now Carnegie Mellon University), particularly the Fine Arts Building, also contain monumental central organizing spaces. The glazing that occupies the three-story-high arches on the Grant and Ross Street facades of the City-County Building also resembles that of Hornbostel's buildings at CMU. In the case of the government building, ingenious walkways with glass floors, sandwiched between exterior and interior walls of glass, cross the central arches at the second and third floors. This innovation, which allows the municipal worker to be poised between views of the city and of the interior hall that is its microcosm, is characteristic of Hornbostel's inventive imagination.

Regardless of these similarities to his past projects, it is Hornbostel's reputation as an extraordinarily innovative architect that has convinced most of the critics who have studied the City-County Building to attribute it to him. History has relegated Hornbostel to the second tier of celebrated American architects. Although well known while he practiced, particularly for his record in winning competitions—"he won more consecutive major national competitions than any other American architect"[18]—today he is not much known outside Pittsburgh. Hornbostel graduated from Columbia University in 1891; from 1893 to 1897 he studied at the École des Beaux-Arts.[19] In Paris, his classmates bestowed upon him the honorary title *l'homme perspectif* for his drawing skills. Back in New York, Hornbostel taught at Columbia, while also working as a partner in a succession of firms. Due to his success in competitions, his practice was national in scope. His better-known works include the architectural accoutrements to New York's Williamsburg, Queensboro, and Hell Gate bridges, and government buildings in Oakland, California; Albany, New York; and Wilmington, Delaware. Besides his campus designs for Carnegie Tech, he designed portions of the campuses at the University of Pittsburgh, Emory University, and Northwestern University. He first came to Pittsburgh in 1904 after winning the competition for the Tech campus, and eventually became the first head of its architecture department. By the time he designed the City-County Building, Hornbostel had established a second base of practice in Pittsburgh.

In at least two ways, Hornbostel's City-County Building is indebted to Richardson's nearby buildings. First, there is the "potent influence" of the Courthouse and Jail mentioned in the newspaper article cited earlier, "preaching the gospel of better architecture" for the city. Richardson's works set such a high standard that they no doubt influenced the government officials in charge of the new building project to organize a design competition in hopes of complementing, if not matching, it.[20] Second, the City-County Building borrows from the Courthouse the arrangement of the monumental arched portals of its facades. Three portals designate the Grant Street fronts of both buildings; a single portal on each responds to the smaller-scale rear facades facing Ross Street. The City-County is also sheathed in granite. Unlike that of the Courthouse and Jail, however, its stone is gray and smooth. There are other significant differences. The City-County is flat-roofed; its side elevations are almost brutally simple, especially since the crossing arcade and grand side entrances shown in the competition drawings were eliminated in the actual building. Whereas the Courthouse was conceived as a monument that would also contain useful spaces, the City-County was a box that emulated commercial office buildings in its massing and exterior appearance.

Edward B. Lee with Palmer, Hornbostel, and Jones (Henry Hornbostel, chief designer), City-County Building, Pittsburgh, Pennsylvania, main elevation on Grant Street. H. H. Richardson's Allegheny County Courthouse is just to the left. Photograph by William Rydberg/Photon.

Like the Courthouse, the City-County occupies an entire city block. However, the two buildings engage their surroundings differently. The City-County Building has an enormous loggia facing Grant Street. The ceiling of this three-story space is vaulted and clad in Gaustavino tile, and its other surfaces, and those of the staircase leading up to it, are of the same gray granite as the building's exterior walls. What the loggia offers, somewhat surprisingly, is a mediating zone between the city and the building's interior great hall. This porch space is just deep enough to gracefully handle the transition from street to interior. This mediating zone has served both as a staging area for community activists and protesters—a place to assemble before proceeding inside—and as an impromptu stage from which politicians can address the public. Indeed, the lower portion of the building's Grant Street facade can be read as a proscenium, facing out to the city. When I worked in the building during the early 1980s, Pittsburgh's popular Mayor Richard Caliguiri would often meet with members of the press in the loggia. Hornbostel created here a secular American translation of the Old World piazza in front of the cathedral. The space is perceptually "outside" to the extent that it seems to belong to the citizenry more than to the municipal government. Yet it is clearly within the sphere of the government's influence. It is the kind of permeable, liminal space that seems to promote exchanges between the potentially hostile parties on either side of it. In contrast, the Courthouse was designed to usher the visitor quickly inside the building and up its grand staircase.[21] The space is imposing and delightfully indeterminate, with its intertwined layers of arches and symmetrically paired runs of stairs. It is, however, an unambiguously interior, controlled space, promoting reverence rather than interaction.

If the covered entry of the City-County Building can be understood as both piazza and porch, the interior space it leads to can just as clearly be considered a street. This great hall extends the length of the building, connecting Grant Street to Ross.[22] The hall is thirty feet wide, and it is topped by a forty-seven-foot-high, barrel-vaulted ceiling. While the loggia creates an indeterminate zone between outside and inside, the interior street attempts to create an idealized "outside." This illusion is possible because the City-County Building contains an enormous light well extending from the second floor through the roof above its ninth floor. The great hall, being somewhat more than three stories tall, protrudes upward into the light well, allowing large clerestories to illuminate the interior street from either side. At the first-floor level, the marble-lined street is flanked by a series of "row offices" that contain the public services most often visited—the register of wills, marriage license bureau, tax office, and so on. These offices form a "solid" base on which rests the bronze classical columns that support the vaulted ceiling. During business hours, indirect light comes through the clerestory windows, reflecting off the columns and into the "street." The sense that one is within an atmospherically comfortable avenue is heightened by Hornbostel's decision to paint the ceiling a deep (sky) blue. While the buildings were designed to satisfy (mostly) different needs,[23] Hornbostel's light-well scheme strikes me as a superior solution to the one Richardson used in the Courthouse. Richardson cleverly daylit his courtrooms, but his exterior light court had no real purpose. Originally a kind of service-yard parking lot for county vehicles, it was used during Prohibition as a stockyard for confiscated liquor.[24] It was not open to the public until 1977, when it was converted into a park, with trees, benches, and a central fountain.

Hornbostel's light well culminates the interior space of the great hall, which allows the City-County Building to channel most of its public movement horizontally. In contrast, the Courthouse's light court is purely exterior, making it (in Pittsburgh's climate) unsuitable as the principal circulation space. The most public interior space in the Courthouse is its monumental main staircase. However majestic this vertical conduit may be, it does not match the easy graciousness of the great hall of the City-County Building, which invites movement. The Courthouse was conceived, to be sure, as less "public" than the City-County Building. Much of the "business" citizens might need to conduct in the Courthouse was required of them by law. In contrast, the lower floors of the City-County have always been a marketplace for government services more likely to attract the casual visitor. My point here is not to claim that one building is superior to the other, but instead to show that it is the City-County, not the Courthouse and Jail, that can teach us more—more that is applicable today—about creating a democratic urban space. If one purpose of the canon is to present us with the finest architectural exemplars, then the City-County Building is at least as deserving of canonization as its famous neighbor.

One indisputable aspect of Hornbostel's talent lies in his manipulation of the public spaces that form the core of most of his buildings.[25]

The boundaries between the public and private zones in a Hornbostel building exhibit a range of permeability. In the City-County Building, the activity within its "street" is, thanks to the transparency of the clerestory, on view to most of the upper-floor offices facing the light court. From within the street, the citizens are aware, through devices such as the glazed walkways noted earlier, of the comings and goings of their public servants. The building is, however, no panopticon. The mostly solid, marble-faced walls of its first-floor offices restrict views perpendicular to the street. This works to reinforce the street illusion, since the angle of view required to look over these offices and through the clerestory is similar to that which someone in an actual street would need to look over the roofs of shops or houses. Hornbostel characteristically creates spaces that are physically distinct but that, due to the vistas they afford to the outside or to other parts of the building, offer a multiple of places for one's gaze. At the same time, his central spaces are never so large as to intimidate. Most architects who have been in City-County's great hall would, I suspect, be surprised to see a drawing of the building's transverse section. The space that dominates the building is actually quite small when seen in the context of the whole building. Hornbostel scaled his public spaces to make them comfortable to those who occupy them. Thus the thirty-foot-wide street has easily accommodated mayoral inaugurations, flower shows, and Christmas pageants, while still permitting people sitting or standing on opposite sides of it to carry on a conversation.

Another reason why the City-County Building offers lessons applicable to contemporary civic buildings, while Richardson's Courthouse and Jail do not, is that the latter buildings are no longer feasible to construct. The era when taxpayers could be persuaded to support the construction of monumental public buildings with the awe-inspiring materiality of Richardson's is long past. The Allegheny County commissioners accepted Richardson's transparently flimsy excuse for his 318-foot-tall "air intake" largely because they wanted the tower as much as he did. Such blissful disregard of economic reality in favor of symbolism we now reserve mainly for the construction of our sport venues. As the architectural historian Joseph Rykwert has written recently, "Dominant buildings have long ceased to be those in which political and public power resides but are rather those of private finance and corporate investment."[26] Although both the Courthouse and Jail and City-County projects faced taxpayer lawsuits aimed at preventing such "wasteful" expenditures,[27] the City-County Building's design strategy is more adaptable to the fiscal realities of the present day.

A mere thirty years separated the construction of the Courthouse and Jail and the City-County Building. Despite this, and although they occupy adjacent sites, they were born into different worlds. In those three decades the Romanesque style Richardson had almost single-handedly popularized had fallen from favor, and the City-County Building had to be constructed against the sobering backdrop of the First World War. H. H. Richardson had intended his two buildings to dominate the Pittsburgh skyline, but in 1901 Henry Clay Frick built his twenty-one-story office building directly across Grant Street from the Courthouse. Thanks to this "great impenetrable slab," the Courthouse tower, "symbol of the majesty of the law," was obscured from most of the city it was designed to face.[28]

In 1904 Hornbostel came to Pittsburgh to design Andrew Carnegie's technical school. While there, he witnessed firsthand the power and arrogance of the city's industrialists. Rather than attempting to compete, Hornbostel gave the City-County Building an anonymous, businesslike exterior. If he could not control the machinations of the city at large, he could plan his building to be a well-ordered virtual city in itself. Into the stark granite box he inserted a self-contained "representative city," a fitting image for a representative urban democracy. Hornbostel then connected the real Pittsburgh to its microcosm through his complaisant loggia, perhaps the ultimate democratic space, where neither civil servant nor civil disobedient could claim sovereignty. It is interesting to note that the models for the great hall and the loggia, that is, the street and the porch, are the public and quasi-public spaces most indigenous to the United States. Perhaps, then, nothing more complicated than the familiarity of their models makes the City-County spaces so well suited to their purposes. The building is, I would argue, unmatched in its gracious accommodation of its citizenry. And yet it is unknown to most architects. In some ways, Hornbostel's strategy worked too well. Eclipsed by the greatness of its neighbors and cloaked in an air of ordinariness of its architect's own devising, the City-County Building remains unnoticed and unappreciated.

At the beginning of the twentieth century, it was still often assumed that architects tended to look like their buildings. Louis Sullivan may have lent authority to this superstition by characterizing Richardson

City-County Building, February 2001. Photograph by William Rydberg/Photon.

and his work as "direct, large, and simple"—although in the case of Richardson, the conclusion was almost inescapable.[29] Boldness and simplicity (of approach, if not form), combined with an identifiable style and expansive physicality, are qualities in both people and buildings that can be readily packaged and consumed. Jeffrey Karl Ochsner has commented upon similar tendencies: "[A]rchitectural historians create narratives that emphasize particular events because they lead to known conclusions. But because this process is selective, the historian of architecture must recognize the inherent tension between the desire to create a structured framework and the desire to recognize and present the more complex and even diffuse context in which design decisions were actually being made. . . . Moreover, that same difficulty is the major impediment to our understanding and appreciating the architecture Richardson influenced. . . ."[30]

Initially, the Allegheny County Courthouse and Jail took their places in the canon with Richardson's other celebrated works because—besides their unarguable excellence—they were big, bold, and among the architect's last works. The Courthouse, not the Jail, was the focus of most of the early publicity, and together the buildings were more widely published than their contemporary, the Marshall Field Store.[31] The Courthouse was often imitated, with the most faithful replicas appearing in Minneapolis, Tacoma, and Los Angeles.[32] Later the Jail became preeminent, in part because it fit an influential narrative, promulgated mainly by Hitchcock, in which Richardson's work "progressed" from the picturesque to the nearly modern. Luckily for Richardson, a bridge joins the two buildings, so the one being promoted at any given time tends to pull the other along with it.

The selective processes of history have been less charitable to the architecture of Hornbostel. All architectural movements direct their harshest criticism to that which immediately precedes them. Thus Modernist critics were mostly unable to recognize the proto-Modern qualities of buildings executed in the style of the École des Beaux-Arts. Hornbostel's reputation has labored under a second difficulty as well. Media attention exhibits a weakness for the visually distinctive,[33] and history for the ideologically pure. Hornbostel's work is neither. Furthermore, the single most defining characteristic of Hornbostel's architecture defies reduction to diagrams or, for that matter, to words. Hornbostel's buildings, whatever they may look like, are all extraordinarily agreeable, kindly, indulgent.[34] Such "immeasurable" qualities are, precisely because they resist transitive measurement, generally excluded from the language of architectural criticism and praise. They are also among the most difficult architectural attributes to replicate,[35] and this, more than any other factor, has limited Hornbostel's influence on later generations of architects.

Many of Richardson's works had similar qualities. Particularly in his smaller structures, such as the Ames Gate Lodge, and in the public libraries, rail stations, and modest churches, one finds the same atmosphere of benevolence. It is much more difficult to inculcate amiability into a project as large as the Courthouse, or as programmatically intimidating as the Jail (although this quality is evident in the Warden's House, built into one corner of the Jail's imposing wall). In the work of Richardson, too, the difficult-to-define qualities that impart humanity to a mute pile of stone have been neglected in favor of other attributes that lead more readily to "known conclusions." It is ironic, then, that if Richardson had any direct influence on Hornbostel, it was most probably through the example of the Marshall Field Store, that darling of Modernist critics. It is also likely that Hornbostel knew of the store's progeny, Louis Sullivan's Auditorium Building (1887–89). In many ways, the massing of the City-County Building is remarkably similar to Sullivan's structure, and each building wraps a distinguished interior space with an anonymous exterior that gives no hint of what lies within.

There are still other connections between Richardson and Horn-bostel. Stanford White was an employee of Richardson's; later on White hired Hornbostel to help in preparing competition drawings for the Military Academy at West Point.[36] Richardson designed the Albany City Hall (1880–82), and, together with Frederick Law Olm-sted and New York architect Leopold Eidlitz, he completed several of the buildings that comprise the New York State Capitol (1876–81).[37] Hornbostel's New York State Education Building sits adjacent to this complex and within sight of the City Hall.[38] Like Richardson, Hornbostel was seldom interested in writing or theorizing about architecture. However, throughout his long career as an educator, Hornbostel was often called upon to judge his own and other ar-chitects' work, and in an article summarizing developments in the Pittsburgh region, he addressed the role of Richardson. "If we must choose one man as the greatest influence in the revival of sound archi-tecture and building in Allegheny County, it is likely that we should choose Henry Hobson Richardson," he wrote. "It is he whom we may thank for the rugged simplicity of our Allegheny County Courthouse and our County Jail. . . . In addition to the two County buildings . . . we have the Emmanuel Protestant Episcopal Church . . . an interest-ing example of Richardson's genius, even in small problems."[39]

By the time this was written, in 1938, Hornbostel had completed so many significant structures in the area that the obvious alterna-tive "greatest influence" on the region's architecture was Hornbostel himself. Awareness of this is possibly betrayed in the less-than-enthusiastic phrase "it is likely that we should choose." Biographical evidence suggests that Hornbostel was as magnanimous as the more famous "H. H." in whose shadow he sometimes stood. It is hard to imagine Hornbostel harboring bitterness toward an architect he so clearly admired. There is, however, one last peculiar connection between the two men—one which suggests that Hornbostel was not above taking a presumably playful poke at his rival. Almost since the Courthouse and Jail were completed, there had been grumbling that the buildings were overcrowded, and before either the City-County Building or the nearby County Office Building was erected, several additions were proposed for the Courthouse itself. The most auda-cious was one of 1907, by none other than Hornbostel. The scheme consisted of a 700-foot-high tower inserted into the courtyard of the building. A perspective rendering appeared in several architectural periodicals of the day. The proposal was not well received, and there is reason to suspect that Hornbostel was less than serious in making it. Just a few years earlier, Hornbostel spoke out in opposition to a more modest proposal to add a mere two stories to the Courthouse; he suggested that a shotgun be used on anyone who wanted to "mar" a building "too perfect to tamper with."[40] This statement, along with Hornbostel's career-long aversion to megalomaniacal schemes, suggests that the proposal was intended as a joke. Still, in an episode that could be a standard psychological case study, Hornbostel briefly imagined that *his* project cast the largest shadow on Grant Street.

However it may have influenced our appreciation of Hornbostel's building, the canonization of Richardson's work has not been without benefit for the architecture of Pittsburgh. The fame of the Allegheny County Courthouse and Jail has repeatedly saved the buildings from indignities far less considered than Hornbostel's attempt at one-upmanship. In 1908, reasonably sympathetic changes to the Jail, designed by local architect Frederick J. Osterling, were completed. A new wing was added and another extended, and the wall around the cell blocks was reshaped to enclose additional area.[41] Some injury was done to the Courthouse by the lowering (1913) and widening (1927) of Grant Street, but for the most part the exteriors of the buildings remain as Richardson had intended. The interiors have not been as fortunate. In the 1970s the ceiling heights of some of the courtrooms were cut in half, to make room for mechanical equipment. Luckily, many of these rooms have since been restored. As early as the 1920s, the Jail began to show signs of obsolescence, and in 1924 a county planning commission recommended demolition. Opposition by local architects prevented the execution of this plan. It was the first of many such reprieves the building would be granted over the next fifty years. In 1973 both the Courthouse and Jail were added to the National Register of Historic Places; three years later they were elevated to the status of Historic Landmarks. Such official recognition dampened the zeal that periodically seized cost-cutting bureaucrats and muckraking journalists to alter or abandon them. New facilities have finally replaced the Jail, but fortunately it has been recycled into the new home of the Family and Children's division of the county court system. This reuse required the removal of all but a few jail cells (kept for display); spatially, the building has been left intact.[42]

The first thing a visitor to the City-County Building is likely to notice today is how poorly maintained it is compared to the corporate towers around it.[43] A patina of cigar smoke seems to cling to the marble of the great hall, and cigarette butts collect in the loggia. But no radical changes have been made to the building. This is a testimony to the longevity of Hornbostel's vision since, unlike the Courthouse and Jail, City-County has attracted no legion of defenders to protect it. It is hard to say whether the building would be more widely known had it not been built in the shadow of the giant next door. As it stands, the City-County Building, together with the countless "background buildings" that are its peers, offers to architects and historians a cautionary tale. The spotlight of canonization is an unsubtle instrument. Like any useful abstraction, it can encourage a kind of intellectual laziness. There will always be, quoting Ochsner again, "an inherent tension between the desire to create a structured framework" of "known conclusions" and the wish to acknowledge "the more complex and even diffuse context" that is the entire field of architectural production. Reconsidering the canon is an exercise we should periodically undertake. To do so, however, requires not only that we question what is included in the canon, but also that we do some poking around in its shadows.

2001

Notes

My sincere appreciation to the following persons, whose help while researching this article was indispensable: Pittsburgh architects James Radock and Anthony Lucarelli; Bruce Padolf, architect for the City of Pittsburgh Department of Engineering and Construction; Sam Taylor, architect for Allegheny County; Walter Kidney of the Pittsburgh History and Landmarks Foundation; Martin Aurand, Archivist of the Hunt Library Henry Hornbostel Collection, Carnegie Mellon University; and most important, the architectural historian Charles Rosenblum.

1. James F. O'Gorman, *Living Architecture: A Biography of H. H. Richardson* (New York: Simon & Schuster, 1997), 9–10.

2. Many who began an architectural education in American universities during the period from the 1950s to the mid-1970s will recall that almost all nineteenth-century architects other than Richardson were dismissed with the damning term "eclectic." This is not to say that Richardson's work was not considered eclectic too, but rather that even those who judged it so, such as James Marston Fitch, would make an exception for Richardson. Fitch wrote that Richardson's output was "till the end eclectic," for its use of "load-bearing masonry modeled after Romanesque precedent." However, "explicitly historic ornament [he] little by little abandoned," and "the pic-

turesque composition of which he was such a master is gradually subordinated to a system of masses and voids which grows directly from extremely rational plans"; James Marston Fitch, *American Building: The Historical Forces That Shaped It* (New York: Houghton Mifflin, 1947; New York: Schocken, 1973), 193–94.

3. O'Gorman, *Living Architecture*, 181.

4. James Van Trump, *Majesty of the Law: The Courthouses of Allegheny County* (Pittsburgh: Pittsburgh History & Landmarks Foundation, 1988). According to citations of Richardson's competition entry text in this volume (54–55), Richardson explained some important features of the design—the lack of "elaborate capitals and carvings" and the reliance on "a quiet and massive treatment of the wall surfaces"—as a response to Pittsburgh's infamous air pollution. Richardson claimed "no dependence for architectural effect is placed upon features liable to be distorted by soot."

5. Ibid., 81.

6. M. G. Van Rensselaer, *Henry Hobson Richardson and His Works* (Boston: Houghton Mifflin Co., 1888; reprint, Park Forest, Ill.: The Prairie School Press, 1967), 92.

7. Richardson completed the Emmanuel Episcopal Church in Allegheny City (since annexed by Pittsburgh) in 1883. Van Trump reports (40–41) that Richardson's firm was not originally among the five invited to submit designs for the Courthouse and Jail. After New York architect George B. Post declined to enter the competition, Richardson was substituted at the behest of influential members of the Emmanuel congregation. Working on the church, Richardson undoubtedly noticed that Pittsburgh was rapidly growing: once it had absorbed Allegheny City, Pittsburgh would rank as the eighth largest city in the United States.

8. For a recent example, see Robert Hughes, *American Visions* (New York: Alfred A. Knopf, 1997), 225–26.

9. Henry-Russell Hitchcock, *The Architecture of H. H. Richardson and His Times* (Cambridge: MIT Press, 1936, 1966), 259.

10. In the opinion of James Marston Fitch, this type of planning was Richardson's true strength: "He was like Roebling and Eiffel in this respect—capable of grasping the large outlines of the problem before him, of analyzing the forces involved, organizing them into a coherent and workable plan"; Fitch, *American Building*, 192.

11. Conventional wisdom has it that Richardson did not write or speak publicly about his architecture. It is true he neither authored any treatise nor offered any "theoretical" explanations. However, the text Richardson included with his courthouse competition reveals that he (and maybe others in his firm) had mastered the rhetoric of design explication. Perhaps sensing that the Pittsburgh selection committee would be composed of practical-minded men, Richardson (as in the examples cited in note 4) portrayed every

aspect of his building's appearance as responding to the unique environment of the city.

12. Van Trump, *Majesty of the Law*, 104.

13. Ibid., 85. The article is from the *Pittsburgh Bulletin*, March 3, 1888.

14. Ibid., 88.

15. "City-County Architect's Plan Chosen," *Pittsburgh Post*, January 20, 1914. Cass Gilbert advised the city and county on the competition and compiled the building program issued to the competing firms. Gilbert's contract (which stipulated that he receive $150 per day plus expenses) is among the documents in the Hornbostel archive at the Hunt Library of Carnegie Mellon University.

16. Van Trump, *Majesty of the Law*, 144; Walter C. Kidney, *Pittsburgh's Landmark Architecture* (Pittsburgh: Pittsburgh History & Landmarks Foundation, 1997), 106. See also Franklin Toker, *Pittsburgh: An Urban Portrait* (University Park: Penn State University Press, 1986).

17. Aymar Embury II, "The Municipal Building, Hartford, Conn.," *Architecture*, February 1916, 25–28; plates XIX–XXXVIII. I thank Pittsburgh architectural historian Walter Kidney for directing me to this possible predecessor to the City-County Building.

18. Harry Sternfeld, *The Golden Jubilee Journal*, Commemorating the 50th Paris Prize Award (1964).

19. Hornbostel's association with Beaux-Arts classicism limited his appeal to the Modernists. Such disinterest could only result from a superficial understanding of Hornbostel's work. Indeed, for a critic such as Hitchcock, Hornbostel's Carnegie Institute buildings, with their Jeffersonian planning, stripped-down Beaux-Arts massing, and building methods inspired by industrial structures, might have been portrayed as precursors to Modernism.

20. In addition, design competitions were very popular at the time and were common for important civic buildings.

21. In this regard, time has been kinder to the City-County Building than to its neighbor. The widening of Grant Street in 1926–29, coupled with the lowering of the Grant's Hill "hump" in 1913, required that the Courthouse entry be relocated from the first floor to the basement. The three great portals have been modified to reach this lower level, so the change has not had much impact on the exterior appearance of the building. However, entering through the low-ceilinged basement (and passing through recently added metal detectors) was clearly not what Richardson had in mind.

22. Actually, the great hall stops short of reaching Ross Street, ending a distance from it roughly equal to the depth of the portico on Grant Street. The hall is thus symmetrically positioned between the two streets, and its ratio of height to length is well suited to a grand gathering space.

23. The first five floors of the City-County Building are devoted to city

and county offices. Courtrooms, judge's chambers, and related support spaces occupy the top four floors.

24. Van Trump, *Majesty of the Law*, 148. In the same volume, in the afterword, Walter C. Kidney reports that Richardson intended horse-drawn vehicles to enter the courtyard and had shown brick paving and a horse fountain in the space (163).

25. Although not an expert on Hornbostel's work, I studied architecture for five years in three different Hornbostel buildings and worked for nearly four years in the City-County Building.

26. Joseph Rykwert, *The Seduction of Place* (New York: Pantheon Books, 2000), 6.

27. Regarding the taxpayer suit against the Courthouse and Jail, see Van Trump, *Majesty of the Law*, 68–69; for the suit against the City-County Building, see "Excavation Started for City-County Hall," *Pittsburgh Post*, July 1915, 2.

28. Van Trump, *Majesty of the Law*, 128.

29. Fitch, *American Building*, 192.

30. Jeffrey Karl Ochsner, "Seeing Richardson in His Time: The Problem of the Romanesque Revival," in *H. H. Richardson: The Architect, His Peers, and Their Era,* ed. Maureen Meister (Cambridge, Mass.: MIT Press, 1999), 103–4.

31. Ibid., 111.

32. Ibid., 127.

33. Note, for example, that critical analysis is almost entirely absent from media coverage of Frank Gehry's buildings.

34. The City-County Building has, for example, gracefully accommodated the political power shift from the party bosses and ward chairmen who once populated its lobby to the department directors who now occupy its corner offices upstairs. During (and before) the administration of Pittsburgh's powerful mayor David Lawrence (1946–62), the various ward chairmen regularly occupied the benches in the great hall of the City-County Building. Since these men held the real political power in the city, citizen complaints, requests, or (literally) "lobbying" occurred in this space. A later mayor, Peter Flaherty, who was elected on a reformist, good-government platform, removed the benches and established his "Mayor's Service Center" in one of the first-floor offices—thus professionalizing duties long dealt with in a more personal and political manner. Although a positive change, it did drain the City-County lobby of some of its energy.

35. One clear demonstration of this is the present condition of the Carnegie Mellon campus. From 1991–99, several new campus buildings, designed by the architect Michael Dennis, were constructed. Despite their careful replication of the massing, materials, and exterior details of Hornbostel's

buildings, the new buildings lack the amiable presence of the originals. Some of this can be attributed to the well-worn familiarity of the older buildings, and some to the differences in construction methods available now. But the rest is a matter of architectural quality.

36. Author correspondence with Henry Hornbostel scholar Charles Rosenblum.

37. O'Gorman, *Living Architecture,* 119.

38. Correspondence with Rosenblum.

39. Henry Hornbostel, "Architecture," in *Allegheny County: A Sesquicentennial Review,* by George E. Kelly (Pittsburgh: Allegheny County Sesquicentennial Committee, 1938), 253.

40. Van Trump, *Majesty of the Law,* 139.

41. Osterling was author of the abandoned proposal for a two-story addition to the Courthouse that Hornbostel and others had protested.

42. Allen Freeman, "Jailhouse Conversion," *Preservation,* January/February 2001, 45–49.

43. "Neglected Landmark," *Pittsburgh Post-Gazette,* May 3, 1998.

6

Eyesore or Art?
On Tyree Guyton's
Heidelberg Project
John Beardsley

In the early hours of November 23, 1991, bulldozers rumbled into Heidelberg Street on Detroit's run-down east side. Their target: four derelict houses that sculptor Tyree Guyton had transformed into giant works of assemblage art. Starting in 1986, with the help of his grandfather and his then-wife, Karen, Guyton had all but obliterated the houses under layers of scavenged materials—tires, hubcaps, broken toys, battered dolls, rusty signs, busted appliances, and automobile parts—all brightened with stripes, polka dots, and random splashes of paint. His actions were an expression of both outrage and art. Then in his early thirties, Guyton had grown up on the street and had watched it decay, as family after family fled in the face of poverty and crime. Abandoned dwellings became crack houses. "You'll think I'm crazy," he said, "but the houses began speaking to me. . . . Things were going down. You know, we're taught in school to look at problems and think of solutions. This was my solution." Disinvestment had made Guyton an urban guerilla, a one-man adaptive reuse program. Perhaps more than he could have imagined, Guyton's actions put him at the center of a clash of values that illuminates the cultural and political complexities of contemporary urban life.

From the outset, Guyton's Heidelberg Project provoked wildly divergent reactions. He became a media sensation—not just locally but

Tyree Guyton, Heidelberg Project, Detroit, Michigan. Photograph by Camillo José Vergara.

nationally. In 1988, his work was featured in *People,* and the next year in *Newsweek* and *Connoisseur.* Guyton received the "Spirit of Detroit Award" from the city council in 1989 for his contribution to metropolitan cultural life. But some of his neighbors complained bitterly. They said his piles of junk were not doing anything to help their already depressed property values, they feared an infestation of rats, and they resented the mostly white suburban art mavens coming to gawk at their neighborhood. Then-mayor Coleman Young came to see the project in the fall of 1991; two weeks later the bulldozers moved in, though numerous other abandoned houses had been scheduled for demolition far longer than those recast by Guyton. The mayor denied ordering the destruction but made no effort to hide his disdain. Exacerbating race and class divisions implicit in the conflict, he suggested that if suburbanites liked the project so much, they should move it to their communities. "Most of those who thought it was art weren't neighbors," he said shortly after the demolition. "They came in from above 8 Mile Road. If they like it so well, build something next door to their own dwellings."[1]

But this is far from the end of the story. Guyton went back to work almost immediately, eventually coating four more houses with salvage and a patina of bright polka dots. The Guyton family place became the "Dotty Wotty House," dedicated to the notion that on the inside we are all the same color. Trees sprouted bicycles and plastic toy cars; vacant lots and sidewalks were strewn with empty suitcases and assorted shoes in homage, said Guyton, to the displaced and homeless. Despite the conciliatory and reconstructive intent of Guyton's work, neighbors, community groups, and city officials continued to object. This past year, the conflict has again reached fever pitch. City officials cited the project with numerous violations, including littering, harboring abandoned vehicles, coloring sidewalks, and operating an illegal junkyard. Despite few outward signs to confirm their view, some on the city council insist that the blight to which Guyton was reacting is a thing of the past. "What he has done . . . spoke to realities at a time that it happened, and that has changed," said Councilwoman Sheila Cockrell, one of Guyton's most active antagonists.[2]

Darci McConnell, a reporter for the *Detroit Free Press* who has covered the project over the years, insists that neighborhood opposition is solid and deep. Echoing Young's position, she says that "most people who support it don't live in the neighborhood, or even in the city. Based on the letters and e-mail I've been getting and neighborhood hearings, the people who are ready for it to go, and who are loudest about it, do live there." Current mayor Dennis Archer, a fan of the project when elected in 1994, has turned ambivalent. "The city of Detroit realizes that the Heidelberg Project has artistic value," he said in a statement. "But it's trying to be sensitive to the concerns of citizens who live in the area . . . especially the senior citizens, and the impact the project has on their quality of life."[3]

Guyton and his critics have different visions for the revival of Heidelberg Street. The artist and his supporters see the project as the focus of an arts district, with a visual and performing arts complex, tourist information center, jazz café, and perhaps community gardens. But another local group, the Gratiot-McDougall United Community Development Corporation, wants a more conventional program, with new and rehabilitated housing, and commercial and retail development. Corporation president Janice Harvey is one of Guyton's severest critics. "Would this project have been tolerated anywhere else for this long? It has created unbelievable pain."[4] As McConnell reports, prospects on both sides are highly speculative. "Whether or not any of this would happen is an open question, as there is no funding in place for either plan." A third option has been floated—to move Guyton's project to another neighborhood. No other district, however, has expressed willingness to take it.

Beaten down by the opposition, Guyton finally agreed in February 1998 to dismantle the project by August of that year. But he let the deadline pass. Buoyed by his supporters, Guyton decided to fight back. On September 21, several hundred gathered on Heidelberg Street, vowing to lie down in front of any city vehicles that might be sent to destroy the project. Two days later, Detroit attorney Greg Siwak filed for and received a temporary restraining order barring the city from taking any action to demolish the project; both sides were ordered into negotiations.

Heidelberg Project Director Jenenne Whitfield argues for its preservation based both on its popularity and on tangible benefits. She says it is the third most visited cultural attraction in the city, after the Detroit Institute of Arts and the Wright Museum of African-American History. She claims a large local following with a substantial national and international audience as well. Demographic analysis of project guest books, provided by attorney Siwak, reveals that nearly 30 percent of visitors come from within the city, two-thirds from Michigan. Nationally, forty-eight of fifty states are represented along with several dozen foreign countries. Whitfield also disputes health and traffic concerns. Four visits by officials from the city department of public health apparently failed to turn up any evidence of rats or roaches. A city planning department study revealed that the streets around the Heidelberg Project are carrying less traffic than they were designed to handle. Further, Whitfield insists the project is having a positive impact on crime. Although it is located in the seventh precinct, an area with the third highest crime rate in the city, she says that no serious incidents have been reported on Heidelberg Street during the life of the project.

City opposition is complicated by property rights issues. Guyton's project sprawls across public and private land; two of the installations are on houses to which the city has claim, but Guyton holds title to the two other dwellings. Guyton's property is apparently somewhat vulnerable because he is behind on taxes, but the Heidelberg Project recently received an anonymous gift to pay off tax debts and to acquire additional lots on which the project is located. While Whitfield says the city's immediate goal is to remove the project from land they own, she insists that their ultimate ambition is to remove it all—even from Guyton's property. Moreover, she is skeptical of their reliance on community opposition, which she insists is not monolithic. Neighborhood children help build and maintain the project;

their families are enthusiastic supporters. She says the Heidelberg area is not really a cohesive community. "People are apathetic. Many are welfare mothers, drug dealers, and old people. They've got other needs. It's not that their opinions shouldn't matter—it's just that art is not on their radar screens." One unintended benefit of this controversy may be to spur broader recognition of the fact that racial and ethnic communities are themselves diverse and harbor as broad a range of opinion as larger demographic groups.

It is hardly surprising that the Heidelberg Project has been a lightning rod for inner-city frustrations. The kind of spontaneous, unsanctioned art created by the likes of Tyree Guyton typically has several audiences, often with distinctly different views. The pattern is the same for other monuments of what might be called "outsider art," including the fabulous shell- and tile-encrusted Watts Towers in Los Angeles, the work of Italian immigrant Sam (or Simon) Rodia, and the Orange Show in Houston, a tribute to the health-giving properties of the orange built by retired postman Jeff McKissack.[5] Opinion about these creations fractures somewhat along class and educational lines, although not entirely. Spontaneous constructions attract an international audience of well-educated art enthusiasts, among whom I number myself. Those who cleave to a notion of art as a critical or transformational practice typically applaud the way "outsider" artists thumb their noses at both artistic and social norms; connoisseurs appreciate the connections in work like Guyton's to a junk aesthetic that can be traced back through assemblage art at least to Kurt Schwitters's *Merzbau*, a profusion of grottolike chambers made by the German artist from salvaged materials in his Hanover house in the decades between the world wars.

Immediate neighbors, who are likely to be unfamiliar with such histories and who have to live with these offbeat constructions, are generally intolerant of them; from a safer distance, they are typically viewed with more curiosity. City bureaucrats, who often regard them as an affront to their authority, are usually the most hostile. In fairness, many unsanctioned creations are of dubious legality: like parts of Guyton's project, they can constitute an instance of artistic "squatting" or occupation of condemned property. City codes and regulations, sometimes in concert with neighborhood opposition, seem to get trotted out in these cases as a justification for city intervention.

Such was the case with an ambitious but ill-fated wooden ark that rose on city-owned vacant land in the ruins of Newark's Central

Tyree Guyton, Heidelberg Project, Detroit, Michigan. Photograph by Camillo José Vergara.

Ward in the 1980s. The creation of a woman named Kea Tawana who worked in the construction trades, the ship was fabricated of scavenged materials; nearly ninety feet long and thirty feet high, it featured a hand-hewn keel and ribs joined by mortise and tenon. Like

Guyton's houses, Tawana's ark was an emblem of resilience and survival in desperate circumstances. But city officials wanted her gone. Though she offered her creation to the city as a community facility and as a museum of shipbuilding techniques, they made her move and dismantle the ark, citing it with many safety and zoning violations. Apparently there is no zoning for arks in Newark.[6]

It is hard not to view this pattern of bureaucratic hostility to underground artists with some skepticism. I wonder if city officials are not motivated more by embarrassment than by sincere concerns for their injured constituents. The attention generated by Guyton and Tawana underscores municipal inability to improve substantively poor neighborhoods. These failures are hardly personal—they are more the result of market forces and demographic trends than bureaucratic indifference. Still, there seems to be little official tolerance for idiosyncrasy, notwithstanding that the harm done by the Heidelberg Project or Tawana's ark pales in comparison to the social inequities caused by disinvestment in the inner cities. As icons of imaginative life, these places strike me as worthy of official sufferance, if not support. Like them or not, they are emblems of resurrection, of the capacity of individuals—arguably even of communities—to re-create themselves from ruins, with or without official involvement.

My own efforts at evaluating Guyton's work express the larger divergence of opinion. On the one hand, as an aging product of the 1960s counterculture, I am cynical of the city's motivation. Why target Guyton when there are plenty of other desperate neighborhoods and plenty of other derelict houses to tear down? As Detroit columnist Heather Newman writes, "If Heidelberg were the last block of abandoned buildings in the city, I could see the logic in talking about dismantling the project to protect property values. But as we all know, it's not. And sadly, it's going to be a long time before it is, which is one of the points of Guyton's art in the first place."[7] Going after Guyton is a diversionary tactic, a cause célèbre for officials with an urgent need for high-visibility accomplishments. On the other hand, the inchoate communitarian in me feels some real sympathy for Guyton's neighbors. They have had to live a long time with another person's peculiarities. In a putative democracy, some attention should be paid to community standards. This is not a simple matter of the artist standing alone against a monolithic community—both sides have energetic and persuasive partisans. Perhaps what is called for is some sort of demographic analysis to determine the majority view—though questions of how the community would be defined and who would be given a voice in this analysis raise potentially insurmountable problems.

As an avowed partisan of the more offbeat forms of cultural expression, I recoil from the notion of art by consensus. If creation has to appeal to a common denominator, it is bound to be dull or normative at best, repressive at worst. As in other efforts to curtail free expression, a compelling state interest needs to be articulated if Guyton is to be silenced—especially on his own property. Instead of hounding him, perhaps the city should draw a line around Guyton's activities, giving him and his supporters an opportunity to buy out the immediate neighbors and letting him get on with his work. Some larger benefit might yet come of it. There is a precedent for the idea that Guyton's project might become a focus for community life. Los Angeles has created an arts center in association with the Watts Towers, and a private foundation, with city help, administers the Orange Show. Houston's cultural life is much the richer for the existence of the Orange Show Foundation: they hire neighborhood kids to help maintain the project, they offer art classes and residencies for artists, and they sponsor the annual Art Car Parade, an armada of outlandish vehicles that has got to be the nation's most amazing show on wheels, invading the city one Saturday morning each April.

Call me a Pollyanna, but if art is valuable at least in part as the inspiration for communication across the frontiers of class and race, then Guyton's work is fabulously successful. Someday, if it happens, I will be sorry to see a project born as an artistic and political manifesto grow into a mainstream amusement. I might then be willing to see Guyton pack his suitcases—and all his other stuff—and move on. In the meantime, the cultural conditions that created the Heidelberg Project remain largely unchanged. Keep on, Tyree Guyton.

1999

Notes

1. Coleman Young, quoted in William Kleinknecht and Patricia Montemurri, "Young Says If Suburbs Like Guyton's Art, They Can Have It," *Detroit Free Press*, 26 November 1991, 2A.

2. Sheila Cockrell, quoted in Darci McConnell, "Artist Agrees to End

Heidelberg Project," *Detroit Free Press*, 24 February 1998, from unpaginated Internet site.

3. Dennis Archer, quoted in Jon Hall, "A Brush with Greatness—and Critics," *Boston Globe*, 7 September 1998.

4. Janice Harvey, quoted in Darci McConnell, "Heidelberg II in the Works," *Detroit Free Press*, 24 March 1998, from unpaginated Internet site.

5. I use the term *outsider* reluctantly; I am aware of its hegemonic implications. For a good analysis of the term, see Eugene W. Metcalf Jr., "From Domination to Desire: Insiders and Outsider Art," in *The Artist Outsider: Creativity and the Boundaries of Culture*, ed. Eugene W. Metcalf Jr. and Michael D. Hall (Washington, D.C.: Smithsonian Institution Press, 1994). On the origins of the term, see my essay "Creating the Outsider" in *Private Worlds: Classic Outsider Art from Europe*, by John Beardsley and Roger Cardinal (Katonah, N.Y.: Katonah Museum of Art, 1998).

6. For more on Kea Tawana's ark, see my book *Gardens of Revelation* (New York: Abbeville Press, 1995).

7. Heather Newman, "So Much to Tear Down; Why Target Heidelberg?" *Detroit Free Press*, 18 September 1998.

7

Toward an Architecture of Humility: On the Value of Experience

Juhani Pallasmaa

Architectural culture, in its social context and core values, has undergone significant shifts over the past half century. When I began my studies in the late 1950s in Helsinki, the heroic Modernist mission still molded architects' collective ambitions. Architecture enjoyed high social status and positive symbolic connotations; architects were seen as the builders of our national identity. Then, beginning in the early 1960s, the postwar ideals of late-Corbusian plasticity and gravitas gave way to structural and modular clarity, prefabrication, transparency, and visual simplicity; Miesian structural classicism and traditional Japanese buildings were inspirations for an architecture of reduction and deliberate anonymity that sought to mirror industrialization.

During the decade following the Paris Spring of 1968, architecture shifted again, becoming politicized; the art of building was scorned as an elitist practice in the service of power; aesthetic yearnings were condemned. The 1980s saw a harsh questioning of Modernist ideology and a renewed interest in formalism. This decade witnessed efforts to reconstruct the identity of the architect, the self-esteem and social role of the discipline; nothing less than a new paradigm was sought.

Today, architects in Finland have largely succeeded in reestablishing a sense of professional identity and mission. And yet the tumultuous changes of recent decades continue to be felt, for the architectural profession has lost much of its prestige as well as its acknowledged position among the shapers of national culture. Indeed, the social significance of the art of architecture is now perilously tenuous. Competition over fees, new quasi-rational practices, the imperatives of cost and speed, and, perhaps most insidiously, the obsession with the image are eroding the soil of architecture.

This brief narrative of the changing values and fortunes of architects in a corner of the world where modern architecture has played an undisputed social role forms the background to my critical views of recent developments. The tendencies I describe, however, are hardly confined to Scandinavia; they appear to be universal, although they vary from place to place. Aware of the dangers of generalization, I believe we must still try to identify cultural undercurrents that inevitably influence architecture. I should acknowledge that many contemporary architects and critics, professional journals, and educational institutions are working to resist the negative influences of our time. Indubitably poetic works of architecture continue to be created in this age of obsessive materialism. And in some sense negative cultural phenomena actually strengthen architecture's humanist mission: resistance to the decay of spiritual and cultural values is now the shared task of architects and artists.

The widespread rejection of the Modernist doctrine, with its emphasis on social morality, has inspired impressive aesthetic diversity, but it has also produced a climate of arrogance, cultural incoherence, and narcissism. As the understanding of architecture as a *social* art has diminished, the idea of architecture as a form of studio art has intensified: contemporary "neo-avant-garde" works are presented today as products of individual genius. And yet paradoxically, artistic authenticity and autonomy of architecture are today being undercut by three cultural tendencies: the commodification of buildings, the self-defeating search for newness, and the hegemony of the marketable image. These cultural tendencies are supported by both commercialized architectural journalism and the voracious global entertainment and tourism industries.

Is architecture relinquishing its potential to embody high-minded cultural and collective values? Is it working to support ideological and commercial brainwashing and exploitation rather than cultural and historical understanding? Is the emphasis on transient construction turning architecture into disposable scenery?

Despite the current critical and media focus on celebrity designer-artists, architecture continues to be that art with the most irrefutable

Renzo Piano Building Workshop, Beyeler Foundation Museum, Basel, Switzerland, 1993–97.
Photograph by Michel Denancé.

and unavoidable grounding in social life. In addition to merely evaluating the aesthetic relevance of individual projects, architectural theory, criticism, and education should survey this now-neglected cultural ground—the *preconditions* of the art of architecture. Both education and practice would benefit from a rigorous cultural analysis of the prevailing state of architecture. What, for instance, is the collective mental background that informs the alarming conservatism— the nostalgic quasi-classicism—of American collegiate and corporate architecture? Is it cultural insecurity? A deeper suppression of the idea of (and hope for) progress? And what kind of mental defenses work to create our sickeningly regressive domestic architecture?

Visual Images

Architectural publication, criticism, and even education are now focused relentlessly on the enticing visual image. The longing for singular, memorable imagery subordinates other aspects of buildings, isolating architecture in disembodied vision. As buildings are conceived and confronted through the eye rather than the entire body—as the camera becomes the ultimate witness to and mediator of architecture—the actual experience of a building, of its spaces and materials, is neglected. By reinforcing visual manipulation and graphic production, computer imaging further detaches architecture from its multisensory essence; as design tools, computers can encourage mere visual manipulation and make us neglect our powers of empathy and imagination. We become voyeurs obsessed with visuality, blind not only to architecture's social reality but also to its functional, economic, and technological realities, which inevitably determine the design of buildings and cities. Our detachment from experiential and sensory reality maroons us in theoretical, intellectual, and conceptual realms.

Haptic Experiences

Recent dramatic changes in the temporal quality of experience have themselves affected architecture, which now must compete, for immediacy of impact, with today's frenetic forms of expression and communication—with fashion, advertising, Web culture, and so on. But while the visual image has an immediate impact, other dimensions of architectural experience require empathy and interpretation, an understanding of cultural and social contexts, and a capacity for envisioning the temporal endurance of buildings beyond momentary fashions. Appreciation of the sensory qualities of architecture requires slowness and patience (this is true for both the design process and the experience and judgment of the finished building). The impact of time, the effects of use and wear, and the processes of aging are rarely considered in contemporary design or criticism. Alvar Aalto believed that the value of a building is best judged fifty years after completion.

The prospect that few new buildings will even last fifty years does not invalidate the significance of time and duration in architectural apperception.

Authentic architectural settings—fully realized microcosmic entities—strengthen our sense of reality; thus, a desire for haptic architecture is clearly emerging in reaction to ocular-centricity. Haptic sensibility savors plasticity, materiality, tactility, and intimacy. It offers nearness and affection rather than distance and control. While images of architecture can be rapidly consumed, haptic architecture is appreciated and comprehended gradually, detail by detail. While the hectic eye of the camera captures a momentary situation, a passing condition of light or an isolated and carefully framed fragment (photographic images are a kind of focused gestalt), the experience of architectural reality depends fundamentally on peripheral and anticipated vision. The perceptual realm that we sense beyond the sphere of focused vision—the event anticipated around a corner, behind a wall, or beneath a surface—is as important as the camera's frozen image. This suggests that one reason why contemporary places so often alienate us—compared with those historical and natural settings that elicit powerful emotional engagement—has to do with the poverty of our peripheral vision. Focused vision makes us mere observers; peripheral perception transforms retinal images into spatial and bodily experience, encouraging participation.

Social Responsibilities

The ocular and hence hedonistic bias of contemporary architecture is exacerbated and in turn intensified by architects' loss of social empathy and mission. Issues of planning, social housing, mass production, and industrialization—all important to early Modernism—are now rarely touched on in publications or academic programs. Modernism sought to respond to the typical and ordinary conditions of life; contemporary elitist architecture favors the unique and the exceptional. This detachment of architectural language from the ground of common experience has produced a kind of architectural autism. Compare, for instance, the fantasy projects so often assigned in studios of the past decade with the socially oriented design problems of the 1950s and 1960s.

Architectural design, as well as writing and criticism, should acknowledge the need for civic responsibility. Architecture should strengthen the reliability and comprehensibility of the world. In this sense, architecture is fundamentally a conservative art; it materializes and preserves the mytho-poetic ground of constructing and inhabiting space, thus framing human existence and action. Through establishing a horizon of existential understanding, architecture encourages us to turn our attention away from architecture itself: authentic architecture suggests images of ideal life.

The mastery of structure and material and the presence of skilled craftsmanship are essential to good architecture. The general weakening of our sense of tectonic reality—a weakening intimately related to the emphasis on surface and appearance—is caused partly by the diminishing role of craft in construction but even more by the growing power of contractors and by the increasing importance of short-term economics at the expense of architectural value. Architecture is too often viewed as a short-lived speculative commodity rather than as a cultural and metaphysical manifestation that frames collective understanding and values. And although projects that question or ridicule this large social role are now celebrated—both avant-garde and corporate projects often emit the fetid air of architectural necrophilia—architecture cannot escape its foundations in real experience. In an age of simulation and virtual reality, we still long for a home.

Continuing Vitality

Despite the general drift toward meaninglessness, some recent work offers glimpses of the continuous vitality of architecture. In so much current building, technology is used merely as a form of visual imagery. In contrast, Renzo Piano designs exemplary structures that combine technological ingenuity with contextual concern and ecological morality. Such work underscores the fact that truly ecological architecture derives from invention and refinement, not from technical or aesthetic regression. The delightful buildings of Glenn Murcutt are elegant blends of reason and modesty, common sense and poetry, technological sophistication and ecological subtlety; they are unique buildings—responses to a particular landscape—with universal applicability. Alvaro Siza's architecture fuses a contemporary formal and spatial complexity with a reassuring sense of tradition and cultural continuity. Sverre Fehn explores the mythical and poetic ground of construction. Steven Holl resensualizes space, material, and light. Peter Zumthor's recent projects convincingly unite opposites: conceptual strength with sensual subtlety, thought with emotion, clarity with mystery, gravity with lightness.

Western industrial culture values power and domination. Referring to a way of philosophizing that does not try to bundle the multitude of human discourses into a single system, Gianni Vattimo has introduced ideas of "weak ontology" and "fragile thought."[1] We can, I would argue, identify a "weak" or "fragile" architecture, or, more precisely, an architecture of the "fragile image," as opposed to the prevalent architecture of strong images. Whereas the latter strives to impress and manipulate, the architecture of fragile image is contextual, multisensory, and responsive. It is concerned with experiential interaction and sensual accommodation. This architecture grows gradually, scene by scene, rather than quickly manifesting a simple, domineering concept.

We can distinguish between an architecture that offers less in its real material encounter than its images promise and an architecture that opens up new layers of experience and meaning when confronted in its built, contextual, and full reality. Visiting a building by Alvar Aalto, for instance, is a richer experience than viewing its image. His works are masterpieces of an episodic architecture that aims to achieve a specific ambiance rather than a formal authority. The paved pathways by Dimitris Pikionis that lead to the Acropolis in Athens, Lawrence Halprin's Ira's Fountain in Portland, Oregon, and Carlo Scarpa's meticulously crafted architectural settings are further examples of an architecture whose full power does not rely on imagery. The work of Pikionis is a dense conversation with time and history; Halprin's designs explore the threshold between architecture and nature; Scarpa's architecture creates a dialogue between concept and making, visuality and hapticity, artistic invention and tradition. Such architecture obscures the categories of foreground and background, object and context; it evokes a liberated sense of natural duration. An architecture of courtesy and attention, it asks us to be humble, receptive, and patient observers.

Focused on visual imagery, detached from social and contextual considerations, much of the architecture of our time—and the publicity that attempts to convince us of its genius—has an air of self-satisfaction and omnipotence. Buildings attempt to conquer the foreground rather than to create a supportive background for action and perception. Our age seems to have lost the virtue of architectural neutrality, restraint, and modesty. Many contemporary architectural projects seem impudent and arrogant. Authentic works of art, however, remain suspended between certainty and uncertainty, faith and doubt. Architectural culture on the threshold of the new millennium would do well to nurture productive tensions: cultural realism and artistic idealism, determination and discretion, ambition and humility.

1999

Note

1. Gianni Vattimo, *The End of Modernity* (Baltimore: Johns Hopkins University Press, 1991).

8

Why Are Some Buildings More Interesting Than Others?

Kurt W. Forster

Any claims we make for buildings that fascinate us and that we find worthy of reflection prove hard to substantiate when our audience has little or no knowledge of the subject or does not incline to our point of view. Being methodical in our effort at persuasion—as I shall attempt to be here—prompts us to adopt a manner of discourse that has become customary in history and criticism, although it may not make us more persuasive as a result: even though the conventions of historical and critical discourse are no less rigorous than those of other disciplines, we tend to preach to the converted or, at least, to the enthusiastic novice. Nevertheless, there is no reason why we should speak about architecture as if it took nothing to grasp the subject or command a personal view, when we routinely concede that people cannot know anything about the stock market, the legal system, or the psychology of delinquents unless they immerse themselves in these subjects. As a first step, we should identify exactly what the object of our fascination is, which traits of a building define its character and suggest connections with the experiences and ideas it elicits. Clarity (of exposition) and knowledge (of history, perception, and thought) are indispensable but hardly sufficient. We depend almost as much on intuition, on hunches we can test, and on a venturesome taste for things we have not set out to find.

Extensive knowledge alone cannot produce serendipitous finds. Occasionally, our hunches lead nowhere, but at other times they help free us of conventional views. Still, extensive knowledge has precious little to do with elitism, and everything to do with the rise in the nineteenth century of the professions and with the complexity of their activities, which has created a world of extreme specialization.

Everyone specializes—as Marilyn Monroe sang so coyly in *Let's Make Love*—not just people like opera singers, manufacturers, architects, and surgeons. Most specialists are specialists because they remain reluctant to share their knowledge with "outsiders." Have you ever met an expert on audio equipment who would stoop to give you a full version of his knowledge? Why should we expect architects and their critics to do what others clearly cannot do without sending us to the library? Perhaps it is because architecture is so omnipresent in our lives that buildings have become our "second nature"—so much so that, affecting us unconsciously, they seem frequently to obscure both nature and our own predicament.

In its mediating role between nature and artifice, architecture is capable of representing natural phenomena and our ever-changing perceptions and images of them. To single out one aspect of this capacity: natural and artificial materials have been employed in diverse ways to "stand in for" nature and artifice. Even after spending more and more of our time in highly artificial environments, we remain amazingly alert to the properties and effects of materials, as if we retained a kind of reptilian capacity to feel, without touching, the warmth of a stone. Idly waiting at a bus stop, we may suddenly notice the effects of weathering and decay on a building we otherwise pass by heedlessly. A brief pause on the street tempts us to reconfigure broken architectural parts and imaginatively reassemble them in an image of their original whole. Much of what we do in such moments relies on sidelong glances and approximations and on memory and imagination, but the inadvertent way a street corner or a campus gateway embeds itself in the mind can tell us much about the potential of architecture. As we recognize how firmly architecture guides our steps, frames our views, and makes material things intelligible, we are more able to gauge the abundance of meanings that emanate from every building. Architecture has become our habitat and therefore—to emphasize the point—one of the principal mediators between nature and human civilization. Where the respective weights of nature and civilization are located in such mediations depends as much on how we construct these notions as on the fabric of architecture itself.

I am hoping to convey how building materials are perceived within a web of ideas and how unusual, even startling, features in their display can challenge our understanding. Some puzzling aspect can make a building resist our usual rush to classify it, until we recognize just how this irritant feature inflects the relationship of nature and artifice. After all, materials can be employed in diverse ways, either to reveal or conceal certain qualities, to impart or repel notions we wish to form of their meaning. As we project our reading on a building, we articulate and continually adjust our interest. The "value" we derive from our perceptions will make our interest in a building wax or wane (and not always in predictable ways). A key monument from the history of architecture may offer us a swift passage to the heart of this matter.

It would have made no sense for Sebastiano Serlio to describe the recently erected Palazzo del Te (1526-34)—Giulio Romano's fabulous estate for the Gonzagas of Mantua—as "a mixture half of nature and half of artifice,"[1] if nature had not meant raw materiality, uncouth labor, and potentially destructive force. "Artifice," on the other hand, is implied in the definitive transformation of materials in accordance with an idea, a work accomplished by means of extreme refinement. Neither nature nor artifice holds full sway over this building; rather, a mingling of the two creates a sense of tension. This tension arises from *discrepancy,* a discrepancy Giulio Romano pushed to paradoxical extremes in his later work. What makes those works paradoxical is that more than one place and several different purposes must be assigned to their component parts for them to make sense, and yet they continue to resist resolution within the logic of the design. Broken pediments with no trace of the forces that fractured them and irregularly placed windows that are nonetheless equidistant from adjacent pilasters are cases in point. The specific character of the Palazzo del Te derives from the incongruous presence of the raw in the refined. The gap between the two also reveals a deepening divide in the ways in which nature was conceived by philosophers and artists, creating an ever-widening breach between observation and explanatory schemes, between intrinsic function and attributed meaning. That contemporary scientific thinking had begun to change fundamental conceptions of human anatomy and the cosmos—to mention only the most revolutionary domains of sixteenth-century science—casts a raking light over the antinomies that Giulio Romano belabored in his architecture. Parallel to the study of human anatomy—called a *fabrica,* an edifice, by Vesalius—in which bones were classified in categorical ways, independent of their local functions, an architectural vocabulary evolved in which new meaning could be constructed by altering architectural syntax and inflecting its idiom.

Where natural processes are being imagined within architecture, they begin to make sense as both radically different from, and rhetorically integral to, their subjugation in artifice. Crude rustication and inexplicable gaps, falling triglyphs, irregular bays, and fantastic decor fall into place in the Mantua palazzo—an architecture that raises the curtain on a novel kind of theater: the spectacle of nature as incessant change, measured by its own limitless time. A fresh look at a Renaissance building like the Palazzo del Te suggests meanings quite different from those prevailing in modern interpretations. Where Ernst Gombrich, Nikolaus Pevsner, and many others in their wake rushed to psychological explanations, seeking the basis of Giulio Romano's design in the (hypothetical) domain of his private feelings and experiences, my reading returns to references current in the architect's time. Responding to these clues, we can examine the conventions of design, its linguistic elements, and their wider implications. These implications bring the significance(s) of those contemporary references to the surface. On this surface of meaning, concepts of nature and fate are bonded to materials and time by means of new combinations. Where rusticated blocks retain an erratic presence within smoothly stuccoed walls, or modest openings cause compressions beneath them, conventional architectural parlance yields to forces outside of its domain.

It would be shortsighted to speak of willfulness, fancy, and insider jokes—although they too have a share in the mix of impressions. What tips the balance in favor of another reading is the emotive power evoked by the cast of architectural characters Giulio brought to the arena of his design. Were he less ingenious in his manipulation, and less inventive in his harnessing of tensions and contradictions (the glue between the fractured parts of his buildings), we might be tempted to dismiss the operation as a piece of effrontery. But because the conjunctions he has created so disarm our logic while engaging our imagination, we vicariously experience the collapse of one world and the adumbration of another. Giulio Romano's architecture demonstrates at once a process of dissolution—as he undermines the architectural assumptions of the early sixteenth century—and a new hypothesis about the very content of architectural design. What surfaces in his designs is nothing less than a *manifestation* of the ever-irresolvable mediation of apparently inert matter and experiential time. Giulio did not simply *translate* a notion that already existed as such in the scientific terms of his day but instead made analogous notions visible and tangible within architecture. This is a step that might provisionally be called an act of imaginative *transmission*.

If I now jump to an altogether different place and time, I do so to make a distinction about the nature of such transmissions by comparing two projects by Peter Eisenman. Both have remained on the drawing board, and both were made for Frankfurt am Main. The first, the 1987 Bio-Center, translated graphic symbols used in genetics into their volumetric equivalents; the second, a 1990 development scheme for an area near the Frankfurt Fairgrounds, subjects a field of nearly half a million square meters to a process of transformation. Whereas the Bio-Center gives a schematic illustration (rationalizing its abstract matrix as a network of functions), the Rebstockhelände actualizes the notion of geological process. The earlier project closes a fairly long search for schematic translations of fixed charts (Romeo and Juliet, 1985; the 1986 University Museum at the California State University at Long Beach); in contrast, the Rebstockhelände is a kind of flowchart. The decisive difference lies in the fact that Eisenman

Eisenman Architects, Staten Island Stadium and Visitor Center, 1998, computer simulation. Courtesy of Eisenman Architects.

abandoned the static types of mapping—which, as it were, freeze-dry any sense of time—in favor of the tracings of precisely their temporal relationships. The key factor in their genesis is time, or rather the times of different processes, not the fixed schemes of their representation. Eisenman sought to surpass an abstract order, whose parts are twice removed from the reality they designate (as in the Bio-Center, where a molecular structure is transcribed into symbols, and these, in turn, are translated into the three-dimensional parts of a building), through an eminently physical manifestation of the imaginary—the imaginary being a landscape *within* the natural setting of the Main Valley, occupied by buildings whose shapes emerge directly from the implied notion of gradually subsiding flux. One sees affinities with the work of the artist Robert Smithson, whose *Spiral Jetty* prompted Craig Owens to observe that "the work appears to have merged physically into its setting, to be embedded in the place where we encounter it."[2] This particular merging does not abolish, however, the dialectic between work and site; on the contrary, it exploits it for "allegorical" ends.[3] We shall need to return later to this prickly term.

The main thread in Eisenman's transformation of his architecture leads us to reflect on natural processes and their representation within architecture. The processes I am speaking about occur almost always within time spans too slow or fast for observation with the naked eye. Through an imaginative leap, and increasingly with the help of technology (such as photography used to capture movement, or CAD software used to "rotate" and illuminate a design), motion is represented as a series of points in time. Recording such processes not only reveals unobservable moments but also imparts an imaginary dimension to them. It could be said that all visualizations (of natural processes) produce new images that are often quite remote from the things they represent. As a celebrated case in point, Marcel Duchamp's *Nude Descending a Staircase* (1912) visualizes movement in a way that would be unthinkable without photographic technology. The advantage of this visual fiction lies in its overlay of moments in time and therefore in its capacity to trace motion. Throughout the century, architects too have sought to deploy stationary elements so as to simulate motion and the flux of time.

As early as his series of houses, Eisenman initiated a process of geometric transformation from an initial split, a separation of the cube from itself. By making a fairly neutral form discrepant with itself, he blocked off the idea of a unitary origin, for one could cling to the notion of the cube's identity only by abolishing the constitutive distance of form from itself. At the very moment when he put his assumptions forward, Eisenman suggested a fundamental cleavage of form from meaning. Dichotomous to the core, his proposition raised an issue within architecture that had come to inform contemporary life in general. From his very first projects, he wanted his architecture to accomplish a transmission between hidden conditions and overt experiences. This recognition could articulate itself in many different ways, as indeed it did when Robert Venturi reacted to the same basic condition by opening the *volière* of historic birds and declaring a new mating season of form with form, indifferent to the meaning of their offspring.

The new options that Eisenman later opened up for his architecture broke with his early iteration of geometries and engendered work of equal internal complexity but even greater significance. The projects for the Reinhardt Haus in Berlin (1992) and the Visitor Center on Staten Island (1998) deploy their structural properties as manifestations of a postindustrial understanding of production. To be sure, the transition from serviceable structure to its image has been amply demonstrated in works by Jean Nouvel, Herzog and de Meuron, and many others. English high-tech architecture paved the way to an imagery that offers a facsimile of its conceptual conditions (even at great structural expense), and the widespread treatment of facades as computer screens—and the corresponding accommodation of functions as if they were the letters of a keyboard—only goes to show that tectonics in its classic sense can no longer be claimed as the fulcrum of architecture. On the contrary, structural mechanics become either invisible (just as typewriters shed their mechanical claptrap and transmogrified into laptops) or transformed into mere rigs on which to suspend the equipment for atmospheric effects.

A building by Herzog and de Meuron is a telling example of such transformations: the electronic Signal Box (designed 1988–89; built 1992–95) in the railroad signal yard at Basel. The architects decided to emphasize the delicacy of its equipment and the distance of the building from the operations it controls by means of an *image*: like a Faraday cage that renders its inside immune to the surrounding electric discharges, the Signal Box is wrapped in horizontal bands of copper. Only toward the middle of each facade are these strips raised like the blades of a vertical blind, allegorizing the jealous protection of the inside while allowing a glance down to the rail yard.

Wrapping a thing to protect it must be one of the oldest activities of our species. In his 1860 book *Style in the Technical and Tectonic Arts,* Gottfried Semper made the point that "the decoration of the strap is partly dependent on its band-like form and should be consistent with this form. Above all, it should remain surface decoration and not disrupt the intent of the strap; it should imitate its function as a band."[4] To the extent that this ancient idea of protecting an object through wrapping is now transposed into the realm of invisible forces, a distant datum of human experience (of nature) is transmitted into architecture.

On the other hand, in Herzog and de Meuron's silk-screened leaf silhouettes on the facade panels of the Shipping Center at Mulhouse-Brunstatt for the Ricola Company (France, 1993–94), the architects merely apply a familiar organic image on a building for a manufacturer of herbal throat drops—this is an instance of a rather mechanical translation of form. When they perform the aboriginal act of wrapping an object they consider exposed to the forces discovered by Faraday, however, the architects suggest something about the invisible workings of electricity and our perception of them. Electrical

Herzog and de Meuron, Ricola-Europa, Production and Storage Building, Mulhouse-Brunnstadt, France. Photograph by Margherita Spiluttini.

currents are harnessed to advanced technical ends, but their housing is still fashioned from one of the oldest textile techniques. As if the ghost of Gottfried Semper's theory had returned in this shroud for electricity, the Signal Box gleams during the day in its impenetrable metallic sheen and coalesces at night into a spectral monolith. No literary tropes and ornamental flourishes are pressed into service in order to effect this *transmission* of meaning.

How could the creation of a mere image—of organic continuity between nature and edifice, in the case of the Shipping Center for Ricola—be considered on a par with the genuine *idea* these architects produced about the functioning of a railroad signal box? As a matter of fact, their exceptional building, which remains as inaccessible to the viewer as it is indispensable to railroad operations, betrays a host of implications about *control* in general, and about its increasing *invisibility,* just when its deployment has reached ever more massive proportions. Never mind the science of Faraday, which is transposed into the infinitely more ancient practice of protective wrapping; never mind the mysterious presence of a metallic hive in the midst of passing trains. Its contents have little rapport with its bulk, and its operations even less with its physical structure; thus an essential enigma remains. This impenetrable quality rewrites the equation of all its functions, invisible and symbolic, and yet preserves a fundamental impenetrability for the traveler's passing glance. The Signal Box assumes the silent presence of a sanctuary in the desecrated terms of our time: what we have harnessed continues to escape our grasp. In its discrepant manifestation as architecture, the Signal Box codifies the powers it seeks to abolish by housing them in an inviolable shroud.

It is impossible to disregard what art has contributed to the making of this building. I would not hesitate to say that it derives much of its impact from a dual transmission: first, by a passage from ancient to modern technology (wrapping to copper banding); second, by extending the compass of contemporary references to include a transition from art to architecture. The Basel art community has long been interested in the work of Joseph Beuys. The former director of its municipal museum, Franz Meyer, was among the first to acquire major works by Beuys for the collection. From their very beginnings as architects, Herzog and de Meuron have made a practice of culling much more from artistic practice than attitude and imagery. The work of Jannis Kounellis and Joseph Beuys left *tel quel* (and telltale) traces in their architecture, even before Herzog and de Meuron began sustained collaborations with artists like the painter Rémy Zaugg. Beuys, moreover, had made inducing current in copper a favorite element of his work. In his shamanistic practices, Beuys enacted the invisible power of electricity in a manner that bears striking resemblance to Aby Warburg's anxious perception of electricity in modern life; in 1923, Warburg, recalling his impressions of America in the 1890s, wrote, "the lightning captured in a wire, captive electricity, has created a culture that puts an end to paganism. What has taken its place? Natural forces are no longer seen in anthropomorphic or biomorphic shapes, but as infinite waves obedient to human touch."[5] One of nature's still mysterious manifestations, electricity, and the high artifice of its domestication, electronics, fuse in the shape of the Basel Signal Box. This building recalls the hypothetical leap of *homo faber* from an instinctual life to a calculating existence as its copper wrapping momentarily gleams in enigmatic silence within the mechanical wasteland of the rail yard.

Herzog and de Meuron thus reconstruct nature and artifice in a manner that holds, balanced, the distinctiveness of each in the difference of the other. Beyond all obvious disparity of building type and historical time, we can still recognize how decisively architectural ideas interact with material conditions and imaginings about their nature. If Giulio Romano's Palazzo del Te could be considered, among other things, as a site of conflict between nature and artifice, Herzog and de Meuron's Signal Box locates an enigma in our own understanding of nature and artifice, of control and fate. Peter Eisenman's concept for the Rebstock site in Frankfurt am Main, on the other hand, inscribes an imaginary geology within the natural one and literally generates buildings from the myriad interferences among the forces he imagines on the site. A clear sign of change in the cultural significance of current architecture is the fact that architects are no longer content to articulate symbols of utility or the mechanics of construction. Other forces, chiefly invisible ones, have begun to manifest themselves through the physical properties and the experiential effects of buildings. A name for these transmitted meanings is hard to find, for they are as inseparable from the material nature and tangible qualities of a building as they are never fully coincident with them. *Discrepancy,* as a condition from which new meaning can emerge, suggests, however, the constructive use to which Craig Owens and others have put the concept of "allegory."

Architecture of every kind answers to purposes, but we also make distinctions between the kind and the quality of purposes. Utility is only one among our expectations, and rarely the main, and indeed never the only purpose. Where architecture merely aligns itself with its own conditions—exhibiting little more than economy, efficiency, and ambition—it fails to mediate between its own material existence and our need to locate ourselves in the world. Only acts of *imaginative transmission* allow us to figure out how we came to fall into the place we occupy and what prospects lie before us. The value we attribute to any building also implies a recognition of imaginative acts. Imaginative buildings speak about the realm of nature as a domain of civilization, not as something infinitely removed or heedlessly replaced, and they engage our senses by means of ingenious inscriptions of many-layered meanings no one can grasp, much less exhaust, at a glance.

1999

Notes

1. Sebastiano Serlio, *Tutte l'Opere d'Architettura* (Venice: Francesco de'Franceschi, 1584), Quarto Libro, fol. 133 verso. Serlio specifically uses the term *interrupted* ("l'architrave, & fregio interrotti") to describe the condition of some architectural members, emphasizing thereby the effects of time and the affinity of the new with ruins.

2. Craig Owens, "The Allegorical Impulse: Toward a Theory of Postmodernism," *October* 12 (Spring 1979): 55. Note that Owens is fully aware of the traditional meaning of allegory as a rather contrived literary and figural device, but that, based on Walter Benjamin's redefinition of the concept in his *Origin of German Tragic Drama,* he suggests its altogether different pertinence to contemporary artistic ideas. His general remark that "in allegorical structure . . . one text is read through another, however fragmentary, intermittent, or chaotic their relationship may be; the paradigm for the allegorical work is thus the palimpsest" is immediately relevant to my reading of the buildings I am discussing below.

3. Cf. Owens, "The Allegorical Impulse."

4. Cited after Gottfried Semper: *The Four Elements of Architecture and Other Writings,* trans. Harry Francis Mallgrave and Wolfgang Herrmann (Cambridge: Cambridge University Press, 1989), 216. A full new translation of Semper's *Der Stil* was prepared by H. F. Mallgrave for the series Texts & Documents, which I instituted at the Getty Research Institute.

5. Aby M. Warburg, *Schlangenritual. Ein Reisebericht*, ed. Ulrich Raulff (Berlin: Wagenbach, 1988), 59. My translation of Warburg differs slightly from Michael F. Steinberg's in *Images from the Region of the American Pueblo Indians of North America* (Ithaca, N.Y.: Cornell University Press, 1995), 54. My own edition and introduction to Aby Warburg's *Collected Writings* is forthcoming in the Texts & Documents series.

9

Questions of Value: An Interview with Kenneth Frampton

William S. Saunders and Nancy Levinson

WILLIAM SAUNDERS AND NANCY LEVINSON: *The idea of artistic genius—of greatness, superiority, the "canon"—has been profoundly challenged in recent decades, judged elitist, irrevocably tied to power and privilege. Is the idea of greatness no longer valid? Are we at a loss to define, however provisionally, what makes for artistic greatness? If so, is this a serious loss or instead a kind of liberation?*

KENNETH FRAMPTON: Irrespective of the issue of elitism that is invariably raised by populists, "greatness" suffers from being difficult to define. The same may be said about "genius," although this is not to say that the phenomenon of genius does not exist. However, the concept of "canon" is a different matter, presupposing the existence of a standard that may serve as either a point of departure or a goal. While a canon cannot be conceived outside the confines of a tradition, neither the canon nor the tradition is fixed. Tradition, in this sense, is not a stable base but rather an evolving referential matrix; a canonical fabric, arising out of the perennial play between tradition and innovation.[1]

Your question may be construed as a critique of the "star" system, one I happen to agree with—although I would be the first to concede that my own writing has sometimes been operative in this regard. Distancing oneself from the star system is certainly liberating, to the extent that, among other things, it helps one to recognize that what ultimately counts is the general level of architectural culture rather than the one-off masterpiece, although the one may be part of the other: thus a single brilliant work may contribute to the general level of the culture, without demeaning the latter through invidious comparison. As I attempted to argue in the last edition of *Modern Architecture: A Critical History,* we have reason to believe that, over the last twenty years, a higher general level of architectural culture has existed in countries like Spain, Finland, France, and Japan, compared with many other developed societies. The reason why this is so varies from country to country. In Spain, it surely existed in large measure because of the power of the *collegio* system: a system of local professional organizations that, until recently, had the power and the capacity to maintain both a standard fee system and some control over building permits, as well as to cultivate critical discourse in the field. In Finland, architecture has played a prominent social role since the foundation of the state; almost every public building there is commissioned as the result of a meticulously organized, open competition system. Similarly, in France, the state has played a large role in the cultivation of new and important architecture.

Why are there such vast differences in the twentieth century between "high" and "low" tastes in architecture, between the buildings esteemed by historians and critics and those embraced by the public?

This split seems to have become particularly exacerbated in the late-modern world, for there were moments, earlier in this century, when there existed convergences between architects' visions and those of society as a whole. One thinks of the realization of H. P. Berlage's Amsterdam South plan between 1910 and 1934, or of the garden city that W. M. Dudok created in Hilversum over the same period. In the United States, one might point to Clarence Stein and Henry Wright's Greenbelt New Towns realized during the New Deal or to Frank Lloyd Wright's innumerable Usonian houses or even to John Entenza's Case Study Houses, which clearly evinced an accessible middle-class vision of modernity in the aftermath of the Second World War. One may argue that the work of Alvar Aalto after 1934 was readily accessible at more than one level, and one may make a similar claim for the best work of Ricardo Legorreta from the mid-1960s on. It would be hard to find a modern hotel that compares to Legorreta's work for the Camino Real chain in Mexico—a powerful, abstract yet hedonistic modern environment that engenders a feeling of luxury without resorting to either kitsch or esotericism. Elsewhere, particularly in Switzerland and Austria, one may point to the continual cultivation of middle-class, low-rise, high-density settlements, from Atelier 5's Siedlung Halen of 1960 to Roland Rainer's development of similar neighborhoods in Puchenau and Linz over the last three decades.

While one can hardly claim that the domestic habitat is the main locus of this split between "high" and "low" taste, it is certainly symptomatic of environmental populism. Any appraisal of consensual environmental culture in the United States has to come to terms with the ubiquitous, free-standing suburban house, which has proliferated due to the interplay of bureaucracy, popular taste, subsidized highways, land speculation, mortgage banking, real-estate speculation, and the habitual modus of American home builders, not to mention the need to maintain the equity of one's home in a highly mobile society. As a consequence of all these forces, we are as far from an ecological pattern of land settlement as ever. A truly democratic, as distinct from a popularly *accessible* modern architecture, would have to achieve some form of low-rise, high-density land settlement, one capable of mediating between the conflicting demands of the individual and the collective. That such a pattern is inimical to the hyper-individualism of the free market is borne out by the current disregard for Serge Chermayeff and Christopher Alexander's 1963 *Community and Privacy*, which, despite their reformist stance, might just as well have never been written. This book postulated low-rise, high-density courtyard housing as an alternative "motopian" suburbia for the American middle class. That this intelligent model failed to take hold of the popular imagination (or of professional discourse) may well be explained by the nature of the introspective court-house typology, so different from the image of the freestanding individual house. In other words, the type failed to produce that one commodity that, in some measure at least, has been imposed on late-modern society by those powerful forces of public relations and advertising that influence our desires, those "hidden persuaders" so aptly characterized four decades ago by Vance Packard.[2]

As part of the critique of greatness, of the "masterpiece," some architects have formulated the concept of "critical" or "subversive" practice, an effort to use the discipline of architecture to challenge prevailing paradigms and power structures. Considered as a form of critique, or cultural action, has this effort been effective? What have been its consequences, intended or otherwise, for the education and practice of architecture?

Most architects engaged in "subversive" practices are hard pressed to declare exactly what they are supposedly subverting. This is perhaps inevitable in a society that seems to possess an infinite capacity to co-opt every overtly radical image or gesture. Thus, contemporary neo-avant-gardism can be defined, almost by default, as a stance that is no longer adversarial.

The radicalism of neo-avant-garde work is confined almost exclusively to form, as we may judge from its indifference to the liberative potential of program. I am not sanguine about the emergence of museums that are indifferent to the exhibition of art, or about the advent of minimalist schools that are indifferent to the scale of the child and to the furnishing of their spaces. What is more, while some contemporary practitioners are able, through facility with computer graphics, to engender "spaces hitherto unimagined" (to use Konrad Wachsmann's memorable phrase), they seem invariably incapable of giving sufficient, if any, indication as to how such spaces might be appropriated by the occupant. Neo-avant-garde work thus favors spectacular aestheticism as a species of autonomous art, graphic in its formation, rather than architecture as such. That this tendency has exercised a strong influence in recent years on both education and practice, particularly in the United States, is only too evident. Eschewing the programmatic and the tectonic to an equal degree, it often reduces the entire undertaking to the morphological. Given its post-Duchampian heuristics and its evocation of chaos theory, etc., this aesthetic speculation is rendered all the more intangible by vague divagations upon the relativity of value in the late-modern world. Such neo-avant-gardism has indubitably yielded an architecture that pertains to the schizophrenic sensibility of our epoch; however, I am doubtful that either education or any form of critique, let alone socially responsible modes of practice, can be predicated on a cultural discourse that is, in the last analysis, so indulgently elusive.

Would you agree that, for much of this century at least, architectural criticism has employed the methodology and approach of art criticism, i.e., it has focused upon the individual creator of architecture and judged works of architecture largely in terms of their formal success? But are criteria and standards used to judge painting and sculpture applicable to a collective and collaborative effort such as architecture?

Since architecture is inextricably mixed up with the life-world, it can hardly be evaluated in the same manner as the other fine arts. In this respect, it should be regarded as a context for culture rather than as any kind of autonomous expression. This brings to mind the ironic aphorism of Alvaro Siza: architects don't invent anything; they transform reality. Or, put another way, architecture is always dependent upon material conditions. It is both deeply involved with reality, and, at the same time, it meditates the effects of reality; extensively determined by pertinent preconditions, architecture nonetheless still possesses the capacity to transform these conditions.

Any criticism worthy of the name should take these factors into account: the aims of the client, and the constraints imposed by building regulations and other limitations ranging from the socioeconomic to the ideological. With regard to this last, I recall that in the late 1960s Giancarlo de Carlo challenged the received idea that housing should be inexpensive by admonishing us to ponder whether housing should, on the contrary, be rather costly. In the same spirit, we might note that much current criticism in the field fails to address, in sensitive ways, the play of climate, the constraints of production, or the sensuous accommodation of the body. Richard Neutra's idea of "bio-realism" was an attempt to respond to such considerations—factors all too easily dismissed by the formalists as being of no relevance to the culture of architecture.

What are the responsibilities of criticism? Or more specifically, of the individual critic? Responsibilities could be defined in terms of the discipline and profession, in terms of the reader, in terms of the work under discussion, etc. In view of such responsibilities, how would you describe the state of contemporary architectural criticism?

Beyond recalling Alan Colquhoun's aphoristic insight that any critique of quality must constantly oscillate between enthusiasm and doubt, I find it difficult to specify the responsibilities of criticism. Criticism must be modulated in light of a particular work, since no universal method can be applied to all works without taking into consideration the subliminal intentions of the work. A truly comprehensive critique ought to be mounted on at least two levels: in the first instance, an assessment of the intentions of the project in relation to its societal context, and in the second, a critical analysis of the building itself in the light of these premises.

It is rare to find examples of contemporary criticism that even come close to these standards. This is partly because today's editors are generally loath to provide space for a truly comprehensive critique. I recall that in the 1950s it was not unusual for a magazine to devote an entire issue to the documentation and evaluation of a single building in all its aspects. More recently, editors have been reluctant to attempt any kind of canonical assessment, in part because of a populist consensus that seeks to please all of the people all of the time, and in part because of a concomitant reluctance to favor any particular line in architectural culture. The exceptions to this have been the "little magazines," such as *Oppositions, assemblage, Modulus, 9H,* etc. Even these, however, have invariably fallen short in terms of documentation, tending to prioritize the written word over either drawing or photographic representation.

The result is that late-modern work has rarely been adequately documented and even more rarely assessed with any rigor. Even those contemporary buildings that do possess true profundity—a dimension of "greatness," in fact—have been, as far as international criticism is concerned, all but ignored. I am thinking, in particular, of a recently completed library at the University of Aveiro designed by Alvaro Siza, certainly worthy of an entire issue of a magazine.

Consider the rapidity with which architectural fashions change, how quickly one taste culture displaces another these days. Consider the widespread, often reflexive desire to be "cutting edge," to anticipate new movements and participate in the very latest developments in design. How does this affect the judging of design? What responsibility does this place upon the critic who wishes to be serious?

Interprofessional competition has perhaps never been more intense, given the deregulation of the architectural profession that happened so long ago that nobody now remembers that professional fees used to be fixed by codes of practice. At the same time, the power of the media is so enormous, at every conceivable level, that one must be on the "cutting edge" in order to receive any attention at all. Needless to say, this so-called cutting edge is given its ephemeral due by a great deal of quotidian writing in the field. This *Candide*-like closure was alluded to by Guy Debord, in his *Commentary on the Society of Spectacle* of 1983, when he wrote: "What is false creates taste, and reinforces itself by knowingly eliminating any possible reference to the authentic. And what is genuine is reconstructed as quickly as possible to resemble the false."

Since we are all subject to the influence of the media, the response to your last question can hardly be sanguine. Even the brightest and the best can falter when the criteria are so contended and the basis of normative practice so enervatingly insecure. It is difficult, to say the least, to maintain the illuminating balance between enthusiasm and doubt that Colquhoun regards as essential to any worthwhile critique. Star architects don't want to be challenged by the unquiet intellect that stubbornly refuses to believe that all is for the best in this best of all pluralist worlds. Clearly, ethical, ecological, psychological, and biological criteria should consciously be reintroduced into our teaching of architecture, without abandoning, as it were, the cultural tradition of the new with which we are all so inextricably involved. Few have addressed this dilemma as persuasively as did Alvar Aalto when he wrote, sixty years ago:

> The structures which were means to create a new architecture have been wrested from us and turned into commercialized decorative ends in themselves with no inner value. There was a time when a misconstrued, lifeless traditionalism was the chief enemy of good architecture. Today its worst enemy is the superficial decorative misuse of the means acquired during the breakthrough. . . . The contrast between deep social responsibility and decorative "surface effects" is perhaps the oldest and certainly the most topical issue in the debate on architecture. Please do not think that I wish to disparage beauty in rejecting decorativeness. Architecture must have charm; it is a factor of beauty in society. But real beauty is not a conception of form which can be taught, it is the result of harmony between several intrinsic factors, not least the social.[3]

More than half a century has elapsed since these words were uttered, and we seem to be plagued still with the same dilemma, perhaps more than ever.

1999

Notes

1. See Hans Georg Gadamer, *Truth and Method*, 2d rev. ed., trans. Joel Weinsheimer and Donald G. Marshall (New York: Continuum, 1993).

2. Vance Oakley Packard, *The Hidden Persuaders* (New York: D. McKay Co., 1957).

3. Alvar Aalto in an interview in the Swedish newspaper *Pagens Nyheter.* See Goran Schildt, *Alvar Aalto: The Decisive Years* (New York: Rizzoli International, 1986), 202–3.

10

Most Architecture Should Be Modest: On Architecture and Aesthetic Judgment

Roger Scruton

What could we possibly mean by "objectivity" in aesthetic judgment? What in particular could we mean by objective "standards" in building and design? These are philosophical questions that I have tried to address in my writings. Here, in summary, is what I think, without the full battery of arguments for thinking it.

Judgments are objective if we are led by our nature as rational beings to agree upon them. This does not mean that those who disagree can be persuaded; nor does it mean that those who agree can find the reasons for doing so. The core principles of moral judgment are objective, even though nobody—not even Aristotle or Kant—has found the final proof of them. They are objective because rational beings, consulting only the facts and setting aside everything that might compromise their impartiality, will come to agree on them. You will agree with your neighbor about the evil of murder, rape, enslavement, or the torture of children, so long as you and your neighbor both put self-interest aside. Those who do not agree with such judgments cannot as a rule be persuaded, but that is because they cannot and will not be impartial.

Something like this is true in aesthetic judgment. About basic matters rational beings have a spontaneous tendency to agree, provided that they attend not to their special and distinguishing interests but to the common concern of everyone. But in such instances it is extremely unlikely that they will disregard their own interests. Those most notorious for rejecting basic principles are those with the heaviest investment in doing so—for example, architects. There is much money to be made from lining city streets with multistory concrete parking garages without facades, such as disgrace the center of Minneapolis. There is therefore a powerful vested interest in the view that there are no objectively valid standards of aesthetic judgment, or in the (equally destructive) view that standards must always be changing, in obedience to social, economic, and technological change.

Subtract the profit makers and the vandals, however, and ask ordinary people how their town should be designed—not for their private good but for the common good—and a surprising level of agreement will be reached. People will agree, for example, on scale: nothing too big for the residential quarters, nothing too broad or tall or domineering for the public parts. They will agree on the need for streets and for doors and windows opening on to the streets. They will agree that buildings should follow the contours of streets and not slice across them or in any way arrogate to themselves spaces that are recognizably public and permeable. They will agree that lighting should be discreet and, if possible, mounted on permanent structures. They will agree on the humanity of some materials and the alienating quality of others; in my view they will even agree about details such as moldings, window frames, and paving stones, as soon as they learn to think of them as chosen not for their personal benefit but for the common good. The classical styles in architecture, in particular the pattern-book vernacular familiar from Beacon Hill, the older parts of Harvard, lower Manhattan, San Francisco, and small-town America, embody this kind of reflective agreement.

To say as much is not to take a stand against Modernism but only to point to matters that Modernists must respect, if they are in their turn to be respected. Martin Heidegger, not otherwise given to lucid utterance, made an important contribution in arguing that "we attain to dwelling . . . only by means of building." He could have put the point the other way round with equal truth: only by learning how to build do we attain to dwelling. Building and dwelling are two parts of a single action. Architecture is the art of settlement. From this simple observation certain principles can be derived that serve to justify those spontaneous patterns of agreement to which I have referred.

The first principle is that buildings should outlast the purpose for which they are constructed. Human purposes are temporary, attached to individual people and their projects; they therefore provide no basis for a collective act of dwelling. Most great buildings have the ability to survive the loss of their original purpose. Sancta Sophia, for example, was a church, a barracks, a stable, a market, and a mosque before becoming a museum. Most houses in our older towns have changed from domestic to commercial use and back again. And even when the purpose of building involves eternity—as in a temple dedicated to the immortals—the purpose will one day be changed. From this it can immediately be seen that functionalism is profoundly mistaken. When form follows function, it becomes as impermanent as function. Like the center of Minneapolis, functional buildings will never lose their disconsolate, stagnant, and temporary appearance, not even if they stand for a century. In architecture function should follow form, as it does in the streets of Bath or Paris or Siena.

The second principle is that aesthetic considerations should take precedence over all others. If we abstract from the present and future functions of a building, and ask ourselves how it should nevertheless be constructed, then we have only one reliable guide: It must look right. Architecture is one of the many areas of social life in which appearance and essence coincide. We should not search behind the appearance to the hidden reality. That which is hidden is of no interest to us. Aesthetic value is the long-term goal; utility, the short-term. After all, nobody wishes to conserve a building if it does not look right.

The third principle is that most users of a building are not clients of the architect. They are the passersby, the residents, the neighbors: those whose horizon is invaded and whose sense of home is affected by this new intrusion. This is why patterns and types are so important. The old pattern books offered precedents to builders, forms that had pleased and harmonized, and that could be relied upon not to spoil or degrade the streets in which they were placed. The failure of Modernism, in my view, lies not in the fact that it has produced no great or beautiful buildings—the chapel at Ronchamp and the houses of Frank Lloyd Wright abundantly prove the opposite. It lies in the absence of any reliable patterns or types, which can be used in awkward or novel situations so as spontaneously to harmonize with the existing urban decor, and so as to retain the essence of the street as a common home. The degradation of our cities is the result of a "Modernist vernacular," whose principal device is the stack of horizontal layers, with jutting and obtrusive corners, built without consideration for the street, without a coherent facade, and without intelligible relation to its neighbors.

Architecture is a public art: whether we like it or not, we are forced to witness it. Until architects recognize that they are altering the dwelling place of everyone, they will be unaware of the nature of their task. You can find proof of this in Boston, where people dwell happily in Beacon Hill and the North End, in streets that have retained their public and genial character, but where whole areas of the town, senselessly redeveloped by Modernist profiteers, are no longer lived in or livable, since the mark of human dwelling has been erased from them.

The fourth principle follows from the last, namely, that architecture is a vernacular art. Although there are the great projects and the great architects who succeed in them, both are exceptions. We build because we need to and for a purpose. Most people who build have no special talent and no high artistic ideals. For them, the aesthetic is important not because they have something special or entrancing to communicate, but merely because, being decent and alert to their neighbors, they want to do what is right. Hence modesty, repeatability, and rule-guidedness are vital architectural resources. Style must be so defined that anyone, however uninspired, can make good use of it and add thereby to the public dwelling space that is our common possession. That is why the most successful period of Western architecture—the period in which real and lasting towns of great size were envisaged and developed—was the period of the classical vernacular, when pattern books guided people who had not fallen prey to the illusion of their own genius.

This does not mean that creativity and imagination have no place in architecture. On the contrary. We depend on the stylistic breakthroughs, the innovations, and the discoveries that create the repeatable vocabulary of forms. Palladian windows, Vignolesque cornices, the classical orders, the Gothic moldings—these great artistic triumphs become types and patterns for lesser mortals. Our best bet in architecture is that the artistic geniuses should invest their energy as Palladio did, in patterns that can be reproduced at will by the rest of us.

This is the true reason why architects should study the orders: not so as to make use of them (although that would be no bad idea) but so as to understand vocabulary and detail. Measurement makes sense only if boundaries are marked. The orders should be understood not as geometrical systems but as systems of significant boundaries—boundaries marked by shadow. In *The Classical Vernacular* I tried to give an account of boundaries that can be generalized to other styles of architecture, and that will show just what should be done by ordinary and talentless builders in order that the rest of us should live happily with their products.

Once we think of architecture as a practice dominated by talentless people, we will come to see how dangerous have been the exultant manifestos and opinionated theories of the Modernists. Millennia of slowly accumulating common sense were discarded for the sake of shallow prescriptions and totalitarian schemes. When architects began to dislike the result, they ceased to be Modernists and called themselves Postmodernists instead. But there is no evidence that they drew the right conclusion from the collapse of Modernism—namely, that Modernism was a mistake. Postmodernism is not an attempt to avoid mistakes but an attempt to build in such a way that the very concept of a mistake has no application. We are living beyond judgment, beyond objectivity, beyond value—so the Postmodernists tell us. How then can we expect architecture to be different?

Such feverish ideas are, in my view, exactly what they seem—self-serving propaganda. Values are objective and permanent; what changes is our ability to believe in them and to make the sacrifices required to live by them. Styles may change, details may come and go, but the broad demands of aesthetic judgment are permanent. By ignoring them we build cities where nobody dwells, cities from which people flee to the suburbs, there to live among leaves and illusions. The American suburb is testimony to the death of architecture—a vast expanse of privatized space where there is no common home and no collective dwelling. For many reasons—environmental, moral, aesthetic, and even religious—it is important that the centrifugal expansion of the city be reversed. People must be enticed again into the city center, to serve as its eyes and ears, to fill it with life and work and leisure, and to make a home amid public and permeable spaces. The case for this has been unanswerably made by Jane Jacobs, but it is never listened to, so powerful are the vested interests that oppose it. That is why it is important that architects understand the objective basis of aesthetic judgment. For they, more than any others, need to be fortified against temptation, in a world where ugliness and destruction earn the highest fees.

1999

11

From Taste to Judgment: Multiple Criteria in the Evaluation of Architecture

William S. Saunders

Context: Relativism and Pragmatism

A verbal judgment of "the value" of some entity—for example, an artwork, a work of literature, or any other kind of object, event, text, or utterance—cannot be a judgment of any independently determinate or, as we say, "objective" property of that entity. . . . [W]hat it can be (and typically is) is a judgment of that entity's contingent value: that is, the speaker's observation or estimate of how the entity will figure in the economy of some limited population of subjects under some limited set of conditions. . . . The "properties" of a work—its "structure," "features," "qualities," and of course its "meanings"—are not fixed, given, or inherent in the work "itself," but are at every point variable products of particular subjects' interactions with it. . . . All normative theories of culture, including those mounted from or in the name of the political left, serve vested tastes and vested interests.
—Barbara Herrnstein Smith, Contingencies of Value, 1988

It does not follow . . . that objective criticism of art is impossible. What follows is that criticism is judgment: that like every judgment it involves a venture, a hypothetical element; that it is directed to qualities which are nevertheless qualities of an object; and that it is concerned with an individual object. . . . [The critic] will realize that his assertion of "good" or "bad" in this and that degree is something the goodness or badness of which is itself to be tested by other persons in their direct perceptual commerce with the object. His criticism issues as a social document and can be checked by others to whom the same objective material is available. Hence the critic, if he is wise, even in making pronouncements of good and bad, of great and small in value, will lay more emphasis upon the objective traits that sustain his judgment than upon values in the sense of excellent or poor. Then his surveys may be of assistance in the direct experience of others.

—John Dewey, Art as Experience, 1934

The Need for Diverse Criteria

First, some assertions about the evaluation of architecture:

- Architecture can be great, good, mediocre, and bad in countless ways. Architecture can and should be judged using many differing criteria. Some criteria are more appropriate than others, depending on the case under consideration; for example, the criteria for an office building must, of course, be different from those for a church.
- More often unconsciously than consciously, we evaluate architecture every time we think, write, and talk about it, even in our choices of what to attend to. When evaluating, we are more trustworthy insofar as we are aware of our usually habitual and temperamental criteria, flexibly test diverse other criteria, and adhere rigidly to no one criterion. (Some criteria, however amorphous, are always operative.)
- The provisional, situationally specific establishment of what

makes for great, good, and bad architecture is an important cultural need, because it is a means of fostering improvement of architecture, and thus, to some extent, of the quality of life.

- The attempt to avoid forming judgments about architecture in the name of relativism, antielitism, distaste for presumptuousness, epistemological skepticism, or simple indifference leads only to self-contradiction (for one does judge anyway) and to aimlessness and egocentrism. It is absurd to argue about preferences; it is absurd not to argue about judgments.

Mere assertions. It would take a book to support them. In any case, you may already know if you agree or disagree. Here, I can only test these assertions through a close look at a few examples of evaluations of architecture.

A vast divide exists between the facile, flippant evaluations—about anything and everything—that so often constitute the sport of our daily conversations, and the careful, principled steering clear of evaluations in formal (mainly academic) writing and speaking. "Objective" historians, scientists, and social scientists stick to "neutral" observation, analysis, and exposition. Yet these same people (along with everyone else) at, say, a cocktail party, let untempered evaluations fly: "Oh, that's such garbage!" "That's the greatest work of the decade!" "Have you every seen anything so ugly?" Criticism is more common than praise.

But suppose one were to blow a time-out whistle and announce: "OK, everyone. In the past half hour, you all have labeled something as very good or bad. You have half an hour to articulate and justify your criteria." I suspect that most people would discover that they are moralistic; that they have some consistent, personal evaluative criteria ("convictions"); that their habitual standards seem, on reflection, too narrow, temperamental, and absolute; and that a desire to feel superior plays a large role in what they say. Important studies could be written by guests who came to parties with hidden tape recorders.

And what if one called time-out and examined implicit criteria in journalistic architectural criticism?

Or at a public review of a design for a city plaza?

At a board meeting held to choose among designs for a corporate tower?

At an architecture school thesis review with a jury of famous architects?

Among developers deciding what house designs to choose for their next tract?

When one is reading a "neutral" architectural history textbook?

In the conversation of a couple selecting a house from among several?

In all these situations, evaluations are expressed more or less carefully and self-consciously. And in all, analyses of judgments would be illuminating—the opportunities for questioning, refining, and changing operative criteria would be vast. What would be most striking, I believe, would be what those evaluating *left out* of consideration, that is, all that their personal traits and histories block them from seeing, much less appreciating.

Yet despite the from-the-gut strength, even dominance, of personal interests and preferences in the evaluation of architecture, architecture, unlike, say, sculpture, quickly forces acknowledgment of multiple, less-personal criteria—agreement prevails that buildings should protect us from harsh weather and meet the functional and programmatic needs of clients.

Beyond these criteria, diverse evaluators—architects, clients, users, passersby, critics, and historians—will usually affirm or discount particular criteria from among the many possible, which include the following: The designed environment should achieve art; create beauty; provide satisfying visual experiences through scale, proportion, balance, rhythm, texture, color, variation, pattern; harmonize function with image and symbolism; be original; blend unobtrusively with its surrounding environment; respond to the character of its region and climate; support and exemplify social/political goals and moral behavior; express the ideals of its community/society; cause no harm to the earth's ecosystem; be well crafted; realize the clients' wants (not the architect's idea of what the client should want); realize the architect's goals; be durable; provide bodily and psychic comfort; achieve its ends economically; achieve good economic return on investment; influence people to visit and return; contribute to high work productivity. One could, of course, go on.

Several of these criteria conflict—they cannot all be upheld at once.

The most common conflict of values in architecture culture seems to be that between individualistic artistry and service to users and

Cover, The Unreal America: Architecture and Illusion.

clients. This debate usually deteriorates into cliché, with most "service" architects scorning "highbrow" architects for their egocentrism, and highbrow architects scorning service architects for their weak creativity. However common this dichotomy may be in practice, it is artificial in principle: the need for aesthetic experience is as real as the need for programmatic efficiency; serving a client's programmatic needs well is a subtle and demanding "art"; artistic buildings can function superbly.

Prevailing Criteria

To explore how conscious and unconscious criteria affect responses to architecture, I will here study criticism by that group of evaluators easiest to "overhear": writers on architecture. After exploring writing by dozens of journalists and academics, I have selected particular writing—by Ada Louise Huxtable, Herbert Muschamp, Mike Davis, Diane Ghirardo, Kenneth Frampton, and Michael Sorkin—because it struck me as especially distinctive and energetic. My wish is not to focus on the writers per se; rather I want to look at samples of the writing and ask, with openness, "what kind of evaluation is going on here?" in order to suggest how varying criteria can limit or enable understanding of architecture, and how such an investigation might lead to a provisional articulation of overarching criteria. My affirmation of a plurality of criteria and my opposition to "Who's to judge? It's all just opinion" relativism are intended to promote self-consciousness, breadth, and flexibility in evaluative responses to architecture.

In the writing on architecture I explored, the criteria that most often emerge are that architecture should

1. be art, should provide a vitalizing, ineffable affective experience through its expressiveness, originality, and formal power and subtlety;
2. be beneficial to the socially and economically underprivileged or, at least, improve the quality of life for any users; and when necessary, resist and provide alternatives to existing abuses of power;
3. revive the "best" traditions of design;
4. be well constructed and use fine materials and craftsmanship; realize tectonic integrity and "presence";
5. allegorically express and/or comment on the spirit of our age and/or the state of our society and culture;
6. embrace, explore, and express the desires and energies of "ordinary" people and vernacular expressions.

More than one of these criteria may, of course, be held simultaneously.

Subjectivism: Huxtable and Muschamp

Ada Louise Huxtable and Herbert Muschamp—in the writing under consideration—hold the first criterion: (their version of) art.[1] As with the other writers, I am selecting discrete samples—in this case Huxtable's "The New Architecture" chapter from *The Unreal America: Architecture and Illusion*[2]—that might not reflect the writer's values elsewhere. "The New Architecture" presents work by (mainly) James Stirling, Frank Gehry, Tadao Ando, Alvaro Siza, and Christian de Portzamparc that goes against the tide of "unreality" Huxtable bemoans throughout the book.

Huxtable here values architecture that provides an intense emotional experience, a "strong visceral sensation . . . a gut response intrinsic to the experience of all great buildings" (150). This position is essentially romantic, supra-rational, grounded in intuitive impressions; it renders evidence and argument secondary. Valuing frisson, this approach treats personal reactions as generalizable: "I feel that this is so, thus it is." Assertion is sufficient when the measure of quality is the positive excitation of a sophisticated sensibility.

The language that seals the book's approbations—language like "unlimited inventive variety . . . not-so-gentle revolution . . . poetic originality . . . dynamic intricacy . . . pure sorcery . . . drama and mystery . . . breathtaking . . . dramatic" (128–65)—is the celebratory language of romanticism. It glorifies the individual genius, the inspired visionary, and our participation in the extraordinary vision. Valuing exuberance of feeling, such a critic has little reason to shade depictions: "[N]o architect has been a more significant agent of change than James Stirling. . . . Stirling was a prodigious talent. No one since has equaled the synthesis of tradition and modernism that he pioneered. . . . His style was so personal as to be inimitable. . . . [H]e reclaimed traditional materials and reshaped historical details for his own purposes—and they were unlike any one else's, at any time" (103–31).

Such absolutism and hyperbole demonstrate the energy of the critic's conviction but at the same time limit debate.[3] In the absence of detailed characterizations of the architectural achievement, one can only respond "I agree" or "I disagree." Since, in this approach, the precise ways that objects prompt (and, ideally, delimit) the writer's feelings and experiences are not of great interest, descriptions can be vague: "To be inside a Gehry house is to experience light, space, and color in a uniquely enriched and expanded way. His best buildings offer perceptions and pleasures hard to imagine before; they provide new dimensions to architecture and living" (141). But just what is the "unique" way? What are the new "pleasures" and "dimensions"?

Cover, New York Times Magazine, September 7, 1997.

The main evaluative adjectives—as in "his buildings have a powerful geometric simplicity" (149)—beg their questions: exactly how and why "powerful"?

This critic defines "those human values which all great architecture serves and turns into art" as "the needs and pleasures of the body and the spirit." The claim seems indisputable. But those "needs and pleasures" are different for different people at different times and places, and they extend outside that which art can offer. If we ask what this approach usually undervalues, we might include the comforting stability that conventional, nonindividualistic, traditional architecture can offer; ecological sustainability; better conditions for the disadvantaged; and availability to many people in many places. In addition, the architecture-as-art position assumes that great buildings spring from one person's brain, whereas, inevitably, given conditions and other people significantly determine what is produced; architects—as they are often painfully aware—have much less control over their work than poets, artists, and musicians.

Herbert Muschamp's "The Miracle in Bilbao" (about Frank O. Gehry & Associates' Guggenheim museum in Spain) displays similarly impressionistic and subjectivistic responses and values.[4] Visiting the museum was giddily exhilarating for the critic: "Bilbao is a sanctuary of free association. It's a bird, it's a plane, it's Superman. It's a ship, an artichoke, the miracle of the rose . . ." (82). One cannot argue, in the absence of direct experience of this museum, that such a response is not warranted—many have found the Guggenheim Museum Bilbao stupendous. One can, however, note how the critic both gives his fantasies free rein and implicitly asserts that buildings that inspire such fantasies are those to be most valued: "The atrium pitches you into an enclosed version of the state of surreality that overtakes you on entering Bilbao," writes Muschamp. "Pinch yourself, but don't wake up. It's better just to dream this" (59).

The critic goes back to his hotel after his first visit to the museum and, from the window, sees a woman on the street, apparently waiting for someone; when he looks back, she is gone. He imagines that she was waiting for her lover and then that she is somehow just like the museum itself—a magical, emotional, ephemeral apparition. Into his associations then pops the thought, "The building I'd just come from was the reincarnation of Marilyn Monroe" (72). Although this may convince us that the writer was enraptured, it cannot convince us that the building is like the disappearing woman or Marilyn Monroe—those responses are too private. "Fools give you reasons" (72), writes this critic, thereby justifying extravagant pronouncements: "If you want to look into the heart of American art today, you are going to need a passport. The word is out that miracles still occur, and that a major one has happened here. . . . It's a real reason to scream. Lose composure. Throw hats into the air. It's a victory for all when any one of us finds a path into freedom, as Frank Gehry has this year in Bilbao, and beyond" (54, 82).[5]

This evaluative method sanctions the honest statement "I like it, even love it," but can articulate only vague criteria, as Muschamp does, quoting others: "What is a masterpiece? . . . 'interpret[ation] of the community to itself' . . . 'continuous working of meaning in the light of the discovery of some truth' . . . 'the myth of the next reality' . . ." (57). It may be that the most inclusive criteria can *only* be quite general, but they need not therefore be vague. Muschamp suggests such a criterion in this essay—"We know what it's like to feel fully alive" (82)—a criterion similar to those that many critics, philosophers, and artists (for instance, John Dewey, D. H. Lawrence, Christopher Alexander, F. R. Leavis) have espoused.[6] More on this later.

It would seem, in sum, that faith in the subjective impressions of one's sensibility is too unreliable a means to judgment.

Politics and Morality: Davis, Ghirardo, Frampton

A second common evaluative criterion is that architecture should demonstrate or support social responsibility through action for the disadvantaged, excluded, controlled, or victimized; in parallel, it discredits architecture that victimizes. Partly in reaction against the aestheticism, formalism, academicism, and zeitgeist representation of the 1980s, this criterion has been advanced frequently in the 1990s by writers as diverse as Mike Davis, Diane Ghirardo, Mary McLeod, Margaret Crawford, and Neil Smith. Finding fault with this value seems impossible: by definition, it's good to be good. The question, as with most criteria, is whether this one excludes other viable criteria and thus undervalues some fine architecture; insistent political pluralism may result, ironically, in narrow judgments about architecture, which, although always political, are always not that alone.

Righteous indignation gives the writing of Mike Davis its power. His *City of Quartz: Excavating the Future in Los Angeles* is a grenade of rage against abuses of power and privilege in his native city, where he sees corruption, greed, callousness, and duplicity everywhere, and thinks despair fully justified.[7] Democracy—especially unrestricted access to a truly public realm—is rare; control, exclusion, and oppression of minorities and the poor are systematized by governments and private security forces. Through this lens, Davis, not intending to be an architectural critic per se, responds to the early architecture of Frank Gehry.

The early Gehry, especially his cheap-material, antibourgeois additions to an existing Dutch Colonial house, might seem compatible

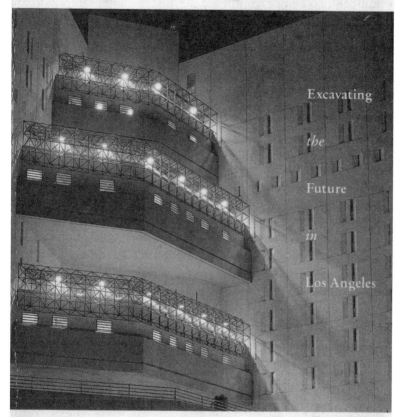

Cover, City of Quartz.

with this writer's values, and indeed at one point we read, "Gehry's strongest suit may simply be his straightforward exploitation of rough urban environments, and his blatant incorporation of their harshest edges and detritus as powerful representational elements in his work. . . . Much of his most interesting work is utterly unromantic and anti-idealistic" (238). If Gehry's work were dedicated just to communicating Davis's own sense of Los Angeles as hell, it would win his full acclaim, even if it did not improve life in the city (only the romantic, in this view, would think it could be improved). But Gehry isn't Davis. Elsewhere we read: "Gehry's work has the peculiar quality of transmuting *noir* into Pop through a recycling of the elements of a decayed and polarized urban landscape (for example, rude concrete, chain-link, empty back walls, and so on) into light and airy expressions of a happy lifestyle (law schools, aquariums, movie libraries, etc.)" (81). "Light and airy expressions of a happy lifestyle"—anything like that would be a travesty for tough and always serious social realism.

The intensity of this kind of political conviction makes its proponent prescriptive: nothing playful, nothing "merely" aesthetic, self-expressive, or innovative will do. The possibility that creating beautiful, funny, and affordable things could be, as Philippe Starck wishes to believe, a political act—helping to uplift the spirits of anyone and everyone—is overlooked. Davis would, it seems likely, disapprove of the Guggenheim Museum Bilbao: the millions spent on an attempt to revitalize a relatively poor and violent region through building a dazzling form rather than through job training, education, nutrition programs, and so on—those millions might represent, to him, the naive belief that a decent life is possible when important material needs are not being met. Exclusionarily, politics can make art seem frivolous, as opposed to another realm with other—usually *not* "light and airy"—goals.

In addition to seeing a "light and airy" Disneyesque frivolity behind Gehry's chain-link, Davis sees Gehry as (at times) "Dirty Harry," cooperating with the exclusionary acts of the privileged against the less privileged: of the 1984 Loyola Law School, he writes, "the radical, or simply idealist, architect might have gambled on opening the campus to the adjacent community, giving it some substantive stake in the design," and he speaks of the "forbidding qualities of the campus's formidable steel stake fencing, concrete bloc [sic] ziggurat, and stark frontage walls." Of the Frances Howard Goldwyn Regional Branch

Library in Hollywood, he writes: "This is undoubtedly the most menacing library ever built. . . . With its fifteen-foot security walls of stucco-covered concrete block, its anti-graffiti barricades covered in ceramic tile, its sunken entrance protected by ten-foot steel stacks . . . [it] projects the same kind of macho exaggeration as Dirty Harry's 44 Magnum. . . . [T]he Samuel Goldwyn Foundation . . . was fixated on physical security. Gehry accepted a commission to design a structure that was inherently 'vandalproof'" (239).

These architectural details certainly seem awful. But, in addition to the hyperbole of "undoubtedly the most menacing library ever built," Davis's comments display a purist's insistence: Gehry was told to design "secure" structures; faced with that fiat, the writer would have preferred that Gehry refuse these commissions. But is Gehry so flatly to be blamed? If he had not accepted these jobs, someone else would have; also, we do not know, from Davis's writing, whether other aspects of this architecture offer socially positive qualities that a lesser architect could not have produced. This writer, in order to approach architecture in all its aspects, would need more openness, an eager-to-be-positive responsiveness, and the ability to value and enjoy ways of acting and thinking different from his own. Although one may (as I do) embrace Davis's political/social values, they blinker him to other values.

Diane Ghirardo's writing, which, like Davis's, is motivated by outrage against classism, racism, sexism, and elitism, is, unlike Davis's, avowedly *architectural* criticism. Two inseparable phenomena repel her: treating architecture as only aesthetic form and ignoring the social, political, and economic realities that surround its production and use. While by no means unresponsive to the aesthetic qualities of buildings, this critic does not believe that architecture is just another art form or that judgments about it as such reflect anything more than socially conditioned tastes. For her, the biased elites of academia and "high design" hold unjustified power and authority to, among other things, exclude nonelite architecture from serious attention.

In "Two Institutions for the Arts," even before experiencing the sensuous forms, materials, textures, and spaces of the Getty Center for the Arts (not yet built), Ghirardo judges the Center, designed by Richard Meier & Partners, based on the social "statement" made by its program and hilltop siting: she calls it "a fantasy of a world apart from the real world . . . one that remains uncontaminated by the mundane preoccupations of the crowded city at its feet" (121).[8]

It suggests "exclusivity and remoteness. There will be no homeless on Getty Center Drive to mar the idyllic landscape" (123). It embodies, for her, a bourgeois fetishism of "white, western European culture . . . wherein the less meaningful the object of artistic attention (such as irises), the more valuable the work, and the greater the emphasis on formal qualities as the measure of the art to the exclusion of other possibilities" (126).

Even if one agrees that the Getty encourages an overly reverential, aloof-from-quotidian-living response to art, one may find in Ghirardo's words some of the dogmatism of social realism, in which "important" subject matter (struggling people, not pretty flowers) is prescribed, as if a painting of irises could not embody (as Van Gogh's does) socially engaged, influential action in the very intensity and rebellion of its painterly vision. There is something formulaic about the critic's lament that the museum is "scrubbed clean of poverty, homelessness, class, race, or ethnic struggle, and even of labor and industrial production" (126)—as if those particular hard realities must always be in focus, and as if some other museums do keep them in focus.

But Ghirardo's treatment of a second museum in this essay—Eisenman Architects' Wexner Center—shows that she can let an open response override her ideology. Despite her well-publicized antipathy toward Eisenman's ideas, actions, and architecture, she allows herself to admire this building: "the Wexner Center does not depend upon the web of obfuscations spun around it, and quite unexpectedly, it is a fine building" (115). But more important, she reveals a refreshingly self-contradictory ("fetishist"?) love for the art and form of architecture—in Giuseppe Terragni's Casa del Fascio, with its "sensitively handled . . . surfaces playing off one another, and with infusions of multiple light qualities" (118) and in Aldo Rossi's arcades, which "extend with a measured, almost timeless dignity, an elegant and majestic backdrop to the promenade . . . articulat[ing] with elegant subtlety different kinds of passageways" (119). If these aren't *aesthetic* responses, I don't know what are.

Like Ghirardo and Davis, Kenneth Frampton believes, in the chapter here under consideration, that the architect's responsibility is primarily to other people and not to the "self" and its expression. But whereas the criticism of Davis and Ghirardo is primarily political, focused on how groups treat other groups, that of Frampton is primarily moral, centered on the quality of life for any and all people. Frampton upholds a "high seriousness" in the tradition of Matthew Arnold.

In "Place, Production and Scenography: International Theory and Practice since 1962," from *Modern Architecture: A Critical History,* Frampton is a moderate, self-effacing, "sensitive and sane" (to use his own phrase, 291) empiricist.[9] His is a commonsensical affirmation of the need for accepting given conditions while attempting to fulfill basic functions and needs (like decent housing), to respond to "the public interest" and ordinary lives, and to respect urban context and nature's ecology. He wants architects to be decent and reasonable socialists. Unsurprisingly, he is repelled by traits he associates with avant-garde and exclusively artistic architecture: self-indulgence, dreaminess, irony, preoccupation with originality, narcissism, introversion, and the production of seductive images, decorations, or populist amusements. Likewise, architecture that springs from arcane intellectualism, ideological dogmatism, or "idiosyncratic obsessions" (Frampton's phrase, 292) fails to reflect the selfless seriousness he thinks crucial. For this writer, serious architecture (for instance, the work of Louis Kahn) demonstrates "two transhistorical conditions of architecture . . . the irreducible nature of tectonic construction and its sublime interaction with light" (302).

Sobriety, realism, selflessness, devotion to others' quality of life and to a civil society—how could one object to such values?[10] The question again is: what do they keep one from valuing that can and should also be valued, perhaps for the very reason that it is not serious and earnestly moral—architecture that is fanciful, poetic, humorous, experimental, populist, abstract, playful, or imagistic in some vital and intelligent way? Perhaps, in the chapter under consideration, the writer is too serious in criticizing (and not at least partially enjoying) Archigram, Reyner Banham, the Centre Pompidou, Las Vegas kitsch, the Piazza d'Italia, and the Staatsgalerie Stuttgart. Critics should, I believe, appreciate capaciously, even as they make judgments that, for instance, what the Piazza d'Italia achieves is less valuable than what, say, the Kimbell Art Museum achieves. They should be willing also to say, "I confess that this kind of architecture is not to my taste, although I recognize its quality; I respect it, but I don't like it."

Pluralism: Sorkin

Although Michael Sorkin's *Village Voice* columns from the late 1970s and the 1980s are occasionally sidetracked by self-regarding efforts to turn clever phrases and be entertaining, they demonstrate, overall, a balanced, flexible, and responsive—yet also fearlessly and fiercely judgmental—architectural criticism.[11] A key measure of the quality of the critical responses is their unpredictability and inconsistency: in turn the critic celebrates functionalism, artistic inventiveness, social responsibility, fitting in, standing out, and so on. Such openness is that of a maverick, independent of cliques, ideologies, institutions, and power/status brokers, immune to hip intellectual and design fads, and free to use effortfully receptive experience as his guide and to be faithful to that experience no matter what hostility and ostracism his judgments might produce.[12]

In a sense it is pathetic to celebrate, as I am, the courage to say what one believes when that might result in exclusion from social circles or even access to some architecture—for how could one expect anything less? Commenting on Philip Johnson's AT&T building, Sorkin says, typically: "Not to put too fine a point on it, the building sucks" (12).[13] However crudely expressed, this judgment reflects a necessary independence. This critic offers his most caustic comments less with gleeful malice than with a weary sense of redressive dutifulness—in fact, he gave up his regular *Voice* column in 1989 because he wearied of finding little to praise in New York architecture (237). Perhaps I admire this criticism because I agree with many of its evaluations. But in agreeing, I am believing (not insisting) that they go beyond mere preferences, since they are borne up by evidence and argument, and they savor qualities in buildings different from those in harmony with the author's spontaneous tastes.

This critic admires Modern architecture in its broadest manifestations—"the technical, the social, the fantastic, the tectonic, the sensual" (4–5)—not as a style but as a way of making. For him, Modernism went wrong in "expunging pleasure, whimsy, joy, or happy irrationality" (2). Contrast this with the Modernist Frampton's greater sobriety and narrower appreciative range—Sorkin's flexibility allows him to appreciate the work of Coop Himmelblau ("spacemen" [348]) and of Paul Rudolph (with its "weight and occasional Roman gloom . . . unabashed grandeur and thickness" [157]), of John Hejduk ("filled with the congenial madness of the romantic" [180]) and Le Corbusier (maker of "a rare and pleasurable place, dignified, bracing, even serene" [252]).

Although his tough-talking, glitz-bashing persona might lead one to expect otherwise, Sorkin's aesthetic appreciations are often deli-

Cover, Exquisite Corpse: Writing on Buildings.

cate: of Aalto he writes, "meticulous to the last detail, his feeling for material and the textures of surfaces is supple, human, and careful. . . . Above all, his work is friendly to people, gracious, never authoritarian. . . . Today's architect is so often the anal retentive or the prig, this kind of sensualism can be embarrassing" (22–25). Sorkin says Aalto "makes beautiful forms useful"—a good summation of a humane Modernism. Although scornful of critic Paul Goldberger's "balance" (his taking *both* sides in debates), Sorkin often modulates his judgments: "de Vaucanson's fowl and Johnson's projects, like the simulations at Busch Gardens and Walt Disney World, simply have no souls. Let's not be too pious about this—I enjoy Disney World and clockwork mallards—but there is danger in them. And that is that they'll finally crowd out the real thing" (177). The caveat "let's not be too pious about this" demonstrates the kind of self-scrutiny that can head off subjectivism.

Perhaps Sorkin's sharpest knife was used to cut through the gussied-up skins of 1980s Postmodernist architecture and reveal the in-no-way glitzy realities of life behind the facade: "For the woman staring at the CRT screen in the windowless back office, whether the doo-dads on the roof are Tuscan or De-Con will be of no great import" (3). "Let's not forget that the activities conducted in those [Las Vegas] casinos are both opiate and rip-off, that their calculation is exquisite. The arty view displaces this manipulation, obscuring it in a schlag of decor" (233). Architecture is important only in its relationship to living.

Ultimately, then, the only criterion steadily maintained in this criticism is so broad as to risk seeming vapid in a New Age kind of way: authentic personal aliveness in the making of architecture—"the eccentricity of individuals . . . the truer comforts of uncertainty. . . . Art, after all, is our great hedge against the oppressions of a universal sure thing" (202). Sensitivity to the dangers of "a universal sure thing" is, I believe, a key trait of good criticism.

Toward Trustworthy Evaluation

So what then, based on this brief tour of varied writing, might an ideal evaluative response to architecture be like? One that begins in an open-minded, open-hearted, generous receptiveness to its object in all its aesthetic, sensory, social, moral, political, historical, environmental, economic, programmatic, and functional dimensions; is aware of the conditions and limitations of the work's production; strives to understand the architects' intentions and the constraints on realizing those intentions; assumes that architecture can and should be judged with many varying criteria and that tests those criteria through a supple, careful apperception of the built work and its broadest context;

respects, acknowledges, and enjoys vastly diverse kinds of architectural achievement; is rigorously self-scrutinizing, wary of its own potential subjective, class, educational, and group biases, and able to reach beyond personal desires and tastes to discover what would be of value to persons quite different from oneself; and finally, prizes architecture that is a manifestation and support of maximum aliveness[14]—the "ur-criterion"—in any of its infinitely diverse manifestations.

An architecture of "maximum aliveness"—to repeat that clunky phrase—is likely to satisfy several (if not most) evaluative criteria at once, or to satisfy one or two criteria to an extraordinary degree. When a building is aesthetically a marvel but functionally weak (or vice versa), the evaluation will give the achievement its full due, yet acknowledge its limitations.[15]

If architecture that achieves significant artistic, affective, inspirational power while satisfying functional needs is that architecture that most embodies fullness and richness of life, then criticism will attend to and celebrate that architecture above all. Having struggled to achieve objectivity and balance, good criticism will not then shy away from citing and characterizing architecture that stifles life or fails to satisfy any more particular reasonable criterion—and from then denunciating and working against it.[16]

1999

Notes

1. There is, one is reminded, a body of literature in architectural criticism and theory that maintains that the functions of architecture are and should be more dissimilar than similar to the functions of "fine art."

2. Ada Louise Huxtable, *The Unreal America: Architecture and Illusion* (New York: The New Press, 1997).

3. Huxtable does, at times, moderate her adulations: of Gehry, she writes, "How far can one go on this particular path without becoming too arbitrary or self-indulgent? . . . Functions can sometimes seem tenuously tied to the idiosyncratic spaces that read as dramatic exterior sculpture. . . . [Gehry] could be seduced by popular acclaim and prodigious publicity into a spectacular stylistic formalism" (164).

4. Herbert Muschamp, "The Miracle in Bilbao," *New York Times Magazine*, 7 September 1997, 54–59, 72, 82.

5. That this mysticism is not exceptional for Muschamp comes through in

this quotation from his review of Richard Meier's Getty Center (*New York Times*, 1 December 1997): "In the late afternoon, the place is a miracle. The great California light spills down on your body, into your eyes. . . . [B]y twilight, you're having a pure Apollo moment. . . . [I]t seems that energy is turning into matter."

6. In, respectively, *Art as Experience,* "Why the Novel Matters," *The Timeless Way of Building,* and *The Living Principle.*

7. Mike Davis, *City of Quartz: Excavating the Future in Los Angeles* (New York: Vintage, 1992); see in particular the "Frank Gehry as Dirty Harry" part of the chapter titled "Fortress L.A."

8. "Two Institutions for the Arts," in *Out of Site: A Social Criticism of Architecture,* ed. Diane Ghirardo (Seattle: Bay Press, 1991).

9. Kenneth Frampton, "Place, Production and Scenography: International Theory and Practice since 1962," in *Modern Architecture: A Critical History* (London: Thames and Hudson, 1980, 1985).

10. Indeed, Frampton may be too confident of the indisputability of his values; this shows up, in particular, in his use of phrases like "of course," "clearly," and "without doubt."

11. Michael Sorkin, *Exquisite Corpse: Writing on Buildings* (London: Verso, 1991).

12. "American architecture is too important to be held prisoner by a bunch of boys that meets in secret to anoint members of the club, reactionaries to whom a social practice means an invitation to lunch, bad designers whose notions of form are the worst kind of parroting"; ibid., 108.

13. Although the word *sucks* has recently replaced the word *stinks* in media discourse, this use in 1978 must have been shocking.

14. "Maximum aliveness" is an attempt to define the broadest and most fundamental possible criterion of value. *Life* is our irreducible condition; to deny it is to affirm nothingness. Those thinkers who have, at times, found "value" in death and nothingness (e.g., Bataille, Freud, Nietzsche, Genet) are, paradoxically and inevitably, affirming a certain quality of life in extremis. "Maximum aliveness" is a phrase that attempts to avoid prescription as to what that aliveness should be; it recognizes and embraces infinite variety in the human comedy. Fine works of art, reaching this standard, may be gloomy or gay, bawdy or puritanical, spiteful or loving (and so on), as long as they have extraordinary vitality (aliveness) in being these things. No lover of architecture would be without Mies van der Rohe's Farnsworth House (evoking clarity, simplicity, economy, and rigor) and Greene and Greene's Gamble House (evoking pleasure in a superabundance of finely crafted details), despite, or in fact *because of,* their vast differences. "Maximum aliveness" is *free* in action, thought, and feeling. The complication in fine architecture is that people are sometimes *forced* to live with another person's "aliveness"—and in those common situations, architecture,

unlike art, demands a moral consideration of other people, and thus self-restraint.

15. Of all critics I am familiar with, the Italian Francisco de Sanctis (1817–83) best exemplifies this mode of generous capaciousness with discrimination. In his *History of Italian Literature,* he values Dante's *Divine Comedy* most highly, as one might expect, yet he is able to fully enjoy and sympathetically characterize the dramatically contrasting achievements of, for instance, the bawdy Boccaccio and Petrarch, the love lyric minimalist.

16. What makes architecture truly *bad*—needing denunciation—as opposed to simply *not good,* would be the subject of long study.

12

Once Again by the Pacific: Returning to Sea Ranch

Tim Culvahouse and Lisa Findley

For those of us studying architecture in the 1970s and early 1980s, the condominium complex at Sea Ranch was a touchstone work. Designed by Charles Moore, Donlyn Lyndon, William Turnbull, and Richard Whitaker—or MLTW, as they were known collectively—and completed in 1966, the project was praised for its harmonious but not self-effacing incorporation of the Northern California vernacular, for its sensitive response to the spectacular Pacific coast, and for its inventive approach to the casual weekend life of well-to-do San Franciscans.[1] Sea Ranch would eventually extend up the coast for ten miles and include countless single-family vacation houses. But it was this first condominium that put the place on the architectural map and suggested rich possibilities for residential architecture in a volatile era marked by the search for new beginnings.

More recently, however, Sea Ranch has almost disappeared from the map; it is no longer on the list of projects likely to be referred to in books, articles, and lectures. It is curious, and perhaps ironic, that the project began to disappear just when it received the Twenty-Five-Year Award from the American Institute of Architects, in 1991. It cannot be found in even so comprehensive a venture as "At the End of the Century: One Hundred Years of Architecture," the millennial exhibition organized by Richard Koshalek and Elizabeth Smith through the

Sea Ranch, Condominium 1, circa 1964. Photograph by Morley Baer. Copyright Morley Baer Trust.

Museum of Contemporary Art in Los Angeles.[2] Nor is it mentioned in books where it would be a natural addition to the conversation, books like David Leatherbarrow's *Uncommon Ground* or Steven Harris and Deborah Berke's *Architecture of the Everyday.*[3] A recent article in the "House and Home" section of the *New York Times* focused on single-family houses at Sea Ranch, mentioning the condominium only in passing.[4] Condominium 1 at Sea Ranch seems no longer to be canonical.

Before considering further the case of Sea Ranch, one might ask: How does a building become canonical? We can think of several ways. First and most obviously, a building becomes canonical when many people admire it. For many Americans, but not for many American architects, the U.S. Capitol is a canonical building, as is the White House. Grandeur, historical and political significance, neoclassical style—these have helped to establish and maintain these famous buildings in the public mind.

For those of us on architecture's professional-academic axis, other criteria might prevail, or perhaps merely other registers of the same criteria. A building's status is as likely to be secured by the grandeur of minimalism as by that of classicism, by the historical and political significance of a building to our profession, by an intellectual, rather than visual, beauty, and certainly by habits of thinking.

We might identify several ways in which a building gains the admiration of architects. One way is originality. Is the building the first of its kind? San Francisco's Hallidie Building holds a minor place in the canon as the first structure with a glass curtain wall. A building may also be canonical for being the last of its kind—witness the Monadnock Block, the last of the skyscrapers with load-bearing walls. A building might be worthy of the textbooks because it seems to epitomize a significant historical moment, as Monticello epitomizes American Palladianism. And a building may be thought to be the best of its kind (one sort of epitome), as the Seagram Building is arguably the best midcentury Modernist high-rise (or, alternatively, the best tall building by Mies).

Or a work may be the most extreme case of a type. If extremity is the principle at work, then the Glass House by Philip Johnson is surely a canonical design. But this strategy does not always work: Johnson's Brick Guest House is as extreme in its own (opposing) way as the Glass House but hardly ranks comparably in the canon. One notable kind of extremity is iconic clarity, an extreme of figural distinction, of which Palladio's Villa Rotunda and Le Corbusier's Villa Savoye are examples.

A building may become canonical not just because it has inherent value, but also because it is readily teachable. Much of Le Corbusier's work qualifies here, as it is easy to diagram and illustrative of articulated and historically differentiated principles (which is not to say that the buildings are not admirable on other terms as well). Richard Norman Shaw's buildings, by contrast, are not so easy to explain, so they are not so fondly taught in design studios; thus, they are not so canonical. Or so one argument might run. A counterargument would hold that the clarity of intention of Le Corbusier's work is precisely what makes the work good—that it makes it easy to teach is merely an added benefit—and Shaw's less clear buildings are simply less good. Finally, a building, once in the canon, may remain there while others fall from view if it continues to yield insights when approached from new critical perspectives. Canonical buildings sustain interrogation.

No doubt there are other reasons a building might be canonized, but we ought fairly to suppose that a combination of groundbreaking originality, crystallization of a historical moment, clear and demonstrable intentions, excellence for its type, a depth that rewards continued attention (and the affection of its users) might secure for a building a place in the canon. If this were the case, there would be no question about the standing of Condominium 1 at Sea Ranch.

And so we believe that the disappearance of Sea Ranch from the map, from the canon, is undeserved—that Sea Ranch merits continuing study and that it is instructive not merely historically but for contemporary practice as well. Its virtues are many. Indeed, like any good poststructuralist project, Sea Ranch is open-ended, nonhierarchical, contingent, and spatially complex, a building in which traditional forms, construction techniques, and spatial ideas have been intriguingly reconsidered. And ultimately, and perhaps most important— since architecture is enclosure for inhabitation—it structures an experience precisely attuned to the lived time of the weekend.

What happened? Why has Sea Ranch receded from view? It is not difficult to imagine why Condominium 1 has recently been neglected within the academy. No doubt this has to do with the subsequent careers of its architects, and particularly with the provocative—some would say kitschy—buildings that Charles Moore designed after he left MLTW: the Piazza d'Italia, the Wonderwall for the New Orleans World's Fair, and so on.[5] William Turnbull followed a more modest path, but if his subsequent projects have earned wide admiration, they have generally been too unassuming to excite critical debate; much the same can said for Donlyn Lyndon's later work. While Richard Whitaker has continued to practice, he has focused more on education.[6]

More is at stake, however, than stylistic preferences for "less" or "more." Condominium 1 reflects the continuing struggle of Modern architects to come to grips with history and with the physical and temporal contexts of architecture. As anthropologist and folklorist Henry Glassie has observed, designers "create out of the smallness of their experience."[7] Within this inescapable limitation, Moore, Lyndon, Turnbull, and Whitaker sought, by combining their various passions, to expand the bounds of Modern architectural practice and to bring to it a renewed formal, spatial, and material generosity. Moreover, in view of the subsequent polarization of architecture into "Modernist" and "Postmodernist" camps, it is worth insisting on the modernity of Sea Ranch. Because of its debt to the regional and vernacular, Sea Ranch has been categorized by some as "Postmodern," and this association, too, has diminished its reputation.[8] But to its designers, although they clearly contributed to the contemporary critique of High Modernist practice, Sea Ranch was in no way a repudiation of Modernist principles. And the critique of High Modernism—which originated within Modernism itself, in the work of Alvar Aalto, Hugo Haring, Sigurd Lewerentz, and others—argued that Modern architecture should not be considered ahistorical and that universalized building forms should not be deployed indifferently from Grenoble to Timbuktu.[9]

The current neglect of Sea Ranch is due partly to the discipline's recent forgetting of these critical propositions. The condominium seems to have disappeared behind Moore's more flamboyant work in much the way that Colin Rowe's historicization of Modern architecture has disappeared behind the cluttering proposals of Rowe and Fred Koetter's *Collage City*.[10] New Modernist buildings are promoted in opposition to the "historical styles," as if once again we believed that the forms of Modernism, alone among artifacts, reside outside history. Recollection of 1920s bungalows is nostalgic; recollection of 1920s *Siedlungen* somehow is not. And Rowe's is not the only criticism we have forgotten; one might think, these last few years, that Alan Colquhoun had never written the essays collected as *Modern Architecture and Historical Change*.[11] Compared with Daniel Libeskind's recent and projected "ducks" (to use Robert Venturi and Denise Scott Brown's term), those of Paul Rudolph have faded like wallflowers into their context.[12] Sea Ranch is, from this perspective, one more victim of architecture's loss of short-term memory. It has been easy, in these Neomodernist days, once again to repudiate the idea of historical style, because so much Postmodernist work recalled historical sources only referentially. A building was to remind you of a Chippendale highboy but not mislead you into supposing that you were actually seeing such a thing. The work that resulted was deliberately devoid of any of those qualities of the original that might serve to ground one in the present—material character, for example, or texture and relief, the play of light and shadow; in this way, it was hoped, it would carry you back more surely to the original. Postmodern historicism has been dissatisfying largely because it has sacrificed the lived experience of the new thing to the recollection of the old.

At Sea Ranch, however, the architects have deployed historical sources not to remind us of those sources (though we may be reminded, and no harm done), but rather to strengthen and shape our immediate experience of the place. The condominium looks to a nearby sheep barn as a material and constructional model, and to the work of Louis Kahn for ideas about the relationship between structure and spatial order. Its spatial composition draws on the concept of the aedicula as described by architectural historian John Summerson,[13] on the idea of the free plan, and also on the idea of the free section, which had been projected but seldom realized in the early years of Modernism. In the shaping of the landscape, too, the designers of Sea Ranch have not only learned from what was there but also incorporated other influences. The landscape planning reflects the designers' careful study of local landforms and of the relationship of vernacular buildings to those forms, but it also uses an idea about "precinct" and "marker" found in William Wurster's Gregory Farmhouse, and a concept derived from the Japanese house about how foreground can work as a miniature landscape. The landscape of the courtyard of Sea Ranch, a steeply tumbling, grassy common space, finds its model in Aalto's Town Hall at Säynätsalo. The automobile court alludes (another instance) to the Gregory Farmhouse, but it also recalls a more nearby model, that of Fort Ross, a nineteenth-century Russian trading post a few miles down the road. Like the fort, Condominium 1 can be viewed as a self-consciously civilized wilderness outpost. As such, Sea Ranch was artfully shaped to accommodate the very particular experience of time and distance that is the city dweller's weekend in the country.

Building

The ways in which MLTW found and used sources for the structure and construction of Sea Ranch tell us much about the eclecticism and transformative energy of their method. The most apparent and thus best-known local source was a sheep barn that still stands on a bluff north of the condominium. (Until the postwar era, this stretch of Northern California coast was occupied mostly by sheep farms.) The architects used the barn as a model, both material and constructional, for how to build in this windswept meadow, but they combined the barn's post-and-beam construction with their own modern understanding of structure. The framing in the barn consists of a series of simple spans—not the most efficient use of wood, since it maximizes bending stress at midspan. In the condominium, the columns are pulled back from the corners in one direction to allow continuous beams to cantilever. In the other direction, another continuous beam spans between both the cantilevers and a single center column. The repeated spatial module, given measure by a structural system that capitalizes on the efficiency of the cantilever, was a lesson learned from Louis Kahn.[14] The cantilever allows a square plan to work as a linear structure; spatially, it accommodates the expansion of the corner into an oblong bay—the strategic, Wrightian dissolution of the corner inflected toward the view. Also, while in the barn the beams span from column to column, in the condominium the beams continue beyond the columns on the outboard side. One critical result is that the siding is separated from the columns by the four-inch width of the beam, which underscores what is only implied in the barn—the distinction between structure and cladding, or between frame and curtain wall. The square structural columns stand clearly separate from the wall, emphasizing the latent modernity of the vernacular.

The free plan of early Modernism, as articulated by Le Corbusier, may have liberated space horizontally; however, when sandwiched between the floor plates of a building, as in the Maison-Domino, it suffered a loss of freedom in section. At the condominium, free plan and free section are combined to create a complex, three-dimensional composition of living spaces within a simple shell. That shell, as we have been arguing, is a Modern one, formed by frame and curtain wall. To our eyes, the bed and bath lofts of Condominium 1 that overlook the main living spaces recall the spiraling spaces of Adolf Loos's *Raumplan,* and it is not difficult to see the spatial development of the condominium complex as a synthesis of Loosian Raumplan and Corbusian *plan libre.*[15] Of course, Loos was not much on the minds of MLTW, or of American architects in general, in the early 1960s. There were, however, other Modern precedents for this sort of disposition of spaces; Lyndon refers in particular to a 1939 project by expatriate American architect Paul Nelson for La Maison Suspendue, in which free-form sleeping pods are hung along a ramp spiraling through a simple, cubic volume.[16]

Each unit of the complex is occupied by diverse, built-in objects that give the spaces both human scale and a sense of expansiveness: a bathroom stacked above an open kitchen, a bay window, a fireplace. Often, a four-columned square loft (one of Moore's beloved aediculae) shelters an intimate space below and forms a bed box above. And if the vocabulary of objects is similar from unit to unit, its deployment is never the same. The architects use a variety of elements to create, within large simple enclosures, complex and overlapping spaces. In this manner MLTW have afforded at Sea Ranch many places in which to be—to sleep, to read, to talk, to have a civilized campout.

The spatial complexity of Sea Ranch anticipates, on the one hand, the current trend in loft living and, on the other, recent morphological experiments. The bohemian style of San Francisco in the 1960s, blended with a deliberately casual version of High Modernism, has here produced double- and triple-height spaces, mezzanine bedrooms, non-programmed living/dining spaces, open kitchens, and large expanses of glass, all of which have come to characterize high-end urban living. The loft, understood as the highly specified occupation of a generic container, has been theorized by Rem Koolhaas in his 1978 *Delirious New York*.[17] OMA's project for Paris's Très Grande Bibliothéque, with its figural volumes suspended in a cubic matrix, is one among many of its latter-day progeny. As an exploration in formal variation, Condominium 1 anticipates as well current investigations into open-ended morphological systems and algorithmic spatial variation, such as those of Greg Lynn.

Unlike many of these investigations, however, the condominium began not with form in the abstract but with concrete conceptions of structure, construction, and inhabited space. MLTW took up the early 1960s fascination with the module, but instead of merely rotating or shifting identical units, as was common practice, they deployed a set of discrete elements—aedicula, kitchen/bath tower, fireplace, bay window—and then disposed them differently in each unit in relationship to the fall of the land, to views, to solar orientation, and to other units. Their method can be seen as "proto-poststructuralist," if by poststructuralism we mean not the presence of certain visual qualities (jarring formal collisions, skewed volumes, Form-Z-generated warped spaces, accelerating curves) but instead the exploration of particulars that set up contingencies, the dismantling of hierarchies, and the opening up of relationships.

Landscape

The condominium's relationship to the landscape is as systematic and as particular as its construction. Its sensitivity to the land is not sentimental. Rather, it suggests the pragmatic yet loving concern of

Sea Ranch, Condominium 1, circa 1964. Photograph by Morley Baer. Copyright Morley Baer Trust.

a farmer for the land: the attitude that land is valuable, possesses its own logic, and can be shaped and used. Buildings designed and made with this attitude have a strong presence in the landscape; they do not try to hide, to blend into the scene. They establish a dialogue. Nestling against the slope of an existing hill, the condominium echoes and in fact accentuates the landforms of the site. Just as Moore would, in later work, develop and refine the kind of spatial complexity he first explored at Sea Ranch, Turnbull would cultivate this sort of conversation with the landscape. It was Turnbull's early diagrams—what the partners refer to as his "Kama Sutra for how to fit the land"—that gave rise to the final clustering of the units.

The landscape armature for the entire Sea Ranch property was the work of landscape architect Lawrence Halprin and included as a central notion the maintaining of cypress hedgerows, planted by sheep farmers as windbreaks, and the planting of new ones. These hedgerows not only eased the wind; they also created, in effect, large, roomlike outdoor spaces between the ocean to the west and the mountains to the east, and thus divided the huge parcel of land into smaller segments. MLTW worked explicitly with this theme of landscape rooms: they distributed the units around two courtyards and gave most private patios. One experiences the landscape at Sea Ranch as a series of nested, enclosed spaces open to the sky and protected from the wind.

MLTW organized the condominium under one shed roof large enough to hold its own against the vastness of the sea and the rocky coastal plain. They chose also to allow the roof slope to generate the building section. At the edge nearest the ocean, the architects set the eave at the lowest height possible; this establishes the low point of the great sloping roof, which echoes the average slope of the site: four-in-twelve. And because the earth does not rise at a regular rate, the volume between the shed roof and the rocky ground varies. It is this variation that allowed the architects to create the intricate spaces in the ten units that make up the complex.

The fit with the landscape continues at other scales. As observant Bay Area architects, MLTW knew of the relentless glare that in the afternoon bounces off the Pacific Ocean. Everyone wants an ocean view, but that view can be unkind, and so the architects provided each unit with an alternate view, up or down the coast, focused on nearer features than the horizon of the Pacific. These middle-ground views also work to anchor the visitor in the landscape, providing a sense of human scale, a place to be, a way to feel grounded at the edge of the limitless sea.

As with the interiors, the relationship between the individual units and the landscape is characterized by inventive variation with a simple palette. The project's south elevation, for instance, which encompasses five units, presents in almost textbook fashion five ways in which the indoors could relate to the outside: with a small fenced court, a balcony, a strip window, a greenhouse, and a sliding door letting directly onto the rocky ground. Almost every unit contains a space level with and opening right onto the ground outside, on the uphill side; the fall of the land leaves the same floor level perched above the ground on the downhill side. This play with topography is overlaid with the play between intimate and distant views. The contrast of outlooks is perhaps most dramatic in Unit 1, where on the uphill side a sliding door opens onto a small, rocky, flat patio shaded by a wind-shaped cypress, while just twenty-five feet across the unit, a bay window two stories above the ground commands a view of the Pacific. What is achieved here is that "simultaneous experience . . . of intense sensations of being inside and outside, of envelopment and detachment" that architect and critic Colin St. John Wilson considers "uniquely the role of the masterpiece."[18]

Weekend

Neither the configuration of the buildings as such—their space, structure, and construction—nor their relationship to the landscape is an end in itself. Condominium 1 is, in essence, a place to be inhabited in a very particular way: as a weekend retreat located at the limit of what most of us would consider a comfortable driving distance from the Bay Area. Condominium 1 must finally be understood as a destination, arrived at with some effort, enjoyed briefly, left reluctantly. This experience and its understanding begin with the journey.

From San Francisco and other Bay Area cities, the hundred-mile trip takes you about two and a half hours, whether you wind over the hills from Healdsburg or twist and turn along the coast on Highway 1. The drive is beautiful, but it is not fast. On either route you encounter the precarious cliffs above the Pacific, the ragged stands of pine and cypress, and the windswept grasslands of the high coastal plain. In this part of California, almost every day, the calm morning air gives way to fierce afternoon winds; the rock-strewn beaches, which all but disappear at high tide, bear little resemblance to the fabled stretches of Los Angeles sand several hundred miles south.

Four decades ago, when Sea Ranch was built, the coastal drive took you through Fort Ross; then, in the mid-1960s, the old trading route that had already become Highway 1 curved through a gap in the palisade of redwood logs, meandered through the fort, and exited through another gap. Slowing for a moment, you were contained by the buildings, sheltered from a landscape that could be as harsh as it was beautiful. You would, in those days, have been aware of how the arrival court of the condominium recalls the courtyard of Fort Ross. That recollection is not possible today, since the highway has been rerouted east of the fort (which is now a state park), but it would have been clear enough to anyone at the time. Less obvious to the layperson (and even to many architects) would be the recollection— noted earlier—of Wurster's Gregory Farmhouse, with its water tower standing sentinel over an entry court, just as the court at Sea Ranch is heralded by the tower of Unit 10. The Gregory Farmhouse itself is part of a regional tradition that derives from the architecture of the Spanish mission: a cluster of buildings surrounding a court, identified afar by its bell tower.

Both the mission and the fort are frontier outposts; each brings civilization into the wilderness. Fort Ross, in its mix of ruggedness and refinement, was, for the designers of the condominium, a telling paradigm of frontier urbanity, of how to make a place in the country intended not for country people but for city dwellers. The fort buildings are constructed of dark, rough-hewn redwood logs, but, in vivid contrast, the windows are finely crafted and whitewashed, evidence that the Russian traders had come from a place more cultivated than the distant country in which they settled. And if in the fort urbanity is suggested mainly in the refinement of the windows, in the condominium it is achieved by the precision with which elements are situated and sequences are developed, a precision that belies the apparent casualness of the juxtapositions. The condominium accommodates the city dweller not symbolically but spatially, making it possible to come to rest in this restless landscape.

Cypresses edge both sides of the short road from the highway to the building. From this shady, fragrant tunnel you emerge into the blinding glare of the afternoon sun. The road then swings left across a meadow, and you enter the first of two courtyards, this one enclosed by tall wooden walls and parking sheds. MLTW's orchestration of automobile entry perceptually prolongs your arrival: by the time you have moved through this series of compressed, contrasting spaces and emerged from your car, you feel far from the highway. Your muscles register the steepness of the site with each trip between car and condo, as you carry in clothes, bedding, firewood, groceries, and wine. The distance between car and condo further distances the visitor from the workaday world.

MLTW have given each unit an astonishing series of small gestures that makes the passage from courtyard to entry hall seem a considerable distance. (This also helps to set up a kind of distance between you and the other, unknown weekenders; you mingle only if you choose to.) Sometimes a gate opens onto a tiny private courtyard; sometimes an intimate short run of stairs ends at a small, enclosed porch; and always the front door is concealed from the courtyard, so that comings and goings are discreet and privacy is maintained.

If you spend only one weekend at the condominium, the unit to rent is Moore's own, number 9. Here, daylight filters from skylights and glows on the wood walls. The aedicula, with bed box above, creates a low, intimate space in front of the fire. On the main level, window seats as wide as single beds flank the bay window, extending out beyond the walls like saddlebags. Let the others take the loft beds and the more conventional bedroom (installed for an ailing Moore shortly before his death). Volunteer for the window seat. There is surely no finer place to wake up in the morning, overlooking the edge of the bluff, with the surf surging around huge rocks where sea lions are also waking, as the mist dissolves and the sun breaks through the fog. And there is no better place to understand the nature of MLTW's work at Sea Ranch.

Observe, for example, the column that intervenes between the main space and the window seat. What might appear to be a happenstance of the morphological system is in fact carefully calculated. The column brings the largest scale of the dwelling—its massive structure—up against one of its most intimate places, emphasizing the extension of the window seat beyond the principal boundary of the enclosure. That enclosure itself, as we have seen, is spaced away from the frame by several inches, reiterating the extension outward. Countering that extension is the thin, taut membrane of glazing that contains you, out beyond the heavy structure, on a light, delicate ledge, just yards from the bluff and the surf below. This place, secure and comfortable, and yet on the edge and also reaching beyond the edge, beckons the moment you arrive.

And that is the crucial moment, the moment you arrive, since the weekend itself is hardly more than an extended arrival, ending in a last-minute departure. It is not only for the sake of the preservation of the landscape that the condominium does not encourage you to spill out onto the lawn with your Weber grill and your Wiffle ball. You have no time for such things. Instead you find, packed into the simple volumes, a complex set of spaces that allows two people to begin a conversation without preliminaries or a half-dozen people to sit down to a meal in a setting that is contained and yet open, obliquely, to the sea. And you find the window seat. The immediacy of these spaces and their expansion into the landscape are the two poles toward which every design judgment was directed. Juxtaposing enclosure and extension, settling you variously but effortlessly into a bracing landscape, the condominium at Sea Ranch gives your weekend a most generous shape.

2001

Notes

1. In 1963, a Hawaii-based developer, Oceanic Properties, commissioned MLTW to design a site plan for several clusters of weekend condominiums on thirty-five acres at the southern end of a five-thousand-acre coastal site. The developer was convinced that the relative density of condominiums would not compromise the sense of "getting away from it all"; well-configured density might help not only to preserve the landscape but also to enhance the experience. Urbane and environmentally responsible, condominiums would concentrate development, and land for open space would be held in common. MLTW's Condominium 1 (the only cluster built to their design), along with the nearby Sea Ranch Lodge (the development's only hotel) and a small group of single-family houses—designed, as was the lodge, by Joseph Esherick—became models for the buildings that would eventually comprise Sea Ranch.

Lawrence Halprin was the master planner. The development of Sea Ranch began at its southern edge, at Condominium 1. Halprin's original concept—that all the houses should tuck up against existing or new hedgerows, leaving the meadows between them open, was realized only in the first few meadows. As the development gained popularity, this strategy was replaced with the more lucrative approach of the typical subdivision.

2. Richard Koshalek and Elizabeth A. T. Smith, "At the End of the Century: One Hundred Years of Architecture," Museum of Contemporary Art, Geffen Contemporary, Los Angeles, 16 April–24 September 2000.

3. David Leatherbarrow, *Uncommon Ground: Architecture, Technology, Topography* (Cambridge, Mass.: MIT Press, 2000); Steven Harris and Deborah Berke, eds., *Architecture of the Everyday* (New York: Princeton Architectural Press, 1997).

4. Diana Ketchum, "A Sea Change Where the View Once Ruled," *New York Times*, May 31, 2001, D1.

5. See, for instance, Kenneth Frampton, *Modern Architecture: A Critical History* (London: Thames and Hudson, 1980), 293. Here Frampton

writes: "The cynicism which ultimately motivates such scenographic operations [as Moore and Turnbull's design for Kresge College at University of California at Santa Cruz] has since been openly conceded by Moore." Frampton then refers to the "flaccid eclecticism of Moore (who abandoned the constructional purity of his Sea Ranch complex . . . as soon as it was completed)." This parenthetical comment is the only mention of Sea Ranch in the book.

6. A recent monograph is noteworthy here: *William Turnbull, Jr.: Buildings in the Landscape* (San Francisco: William Stout Publishers, 2001). Also, several houses by Donlyn Lyndon are featured in the *New York Times* article cited in endnote 4.

7. Henry W. Glassie, *Vernacular Architecture* (Bloomington: University of Indiana Press, 2000), 17. Glassie's earlier *Folk Housing in Middle Virginia* (Knoxville: University of Tennessee Press, 1975) is perhaps unsurpassed as an example of rigorous structural analysis of architecture.

8. Such distinctions may be made too casually and unreflectively, prompted, for example, by what Donlyn Lyndon refers to as "the dumbfoundingly stupid idea that roofs with shapes aren't modern."

9. For this critique within Modernism, see Colin St. John Wilson, *The Other Tradition of Modern Architecture: The Uncompleted Project* (London: Academy Editions, 1995), which expands on earlier essays collected in *Architectural Reflections: Studies in the Philosophy and Practice of Architecture* (Oxford: Butterworth-Heinemann, 1992).

10. See, for the former, Colin Rowe, *The Mathematics of the Ideal Villa* (Cambridge, Mass.: MIT Press, 1976); and, for the latter, Colin Rowe and Frederick Koetter, *Collage City* (Cambridge, Mass.: MIT Press, 1979).

11. Alan Colquhoun, *Essays in Architectural Criticism: Modern Architecture and Historical Change* (Cambridge, Mass.: MIT Press, 1981).

12. Robert Venturi, Denise Scott Brown, and Steven Izenour, *Learning from Las Vegas,* rev. ed. (Cambridge, Mass.: MIT Press, 1977), 87–103.

13. John Summerson, *Heavenly Mansions* (New York: W. W. Norton & Company, 1963).

14. Compare, for example, the plan of Condominium 1 with that of Kahn's Richards Medical Research Laboratory of 1961.

15. For a comparison of the two spatial conceptions, see Max Risselada, ed., *Raumplan versus Plan Libre: Adolf Loos and Le Corbusier, 1919–1930* (New York: Rizzoli, 1991).

16. *La Maison suspendue: recherche de Paul Nelson* (Paris: Éditions Albert Morancé, 1939).

17. Rem Koolhaas, *Delirious New York* (New York: Oxford University Press, 1978).

18. Wilson, *Architectural Reflections,* 8. Wilson applies here to architecture concepts originally developed by Adrian Stokes for painting.

13

The Absence of Presence: The Knickerbocker Residence and the Fate of Nonelitist Architecture

Diane Ghirardo

> If one doesn't talk about a thing, it has never happened.
> —Oscar Wilde, *The Picture of Dorian Gray*

What accounts for the renown of some buildings, even when they suffer significant problems, and the obscurity of many other buildings of great merit, not to mention greater physical integrity? This question presented itself urgently as I stood in the Schindler House in Los Angeles on a rainy day in January. Strategically placed buckets caught the rainwater that streamed down from various leaks, and even the furiously burning fireplaces and the press of many bodies failed to relieve the bone-chilling cold. Surely the fame of this building came only at the price of ignoring serious problems. Since I can find no substantive justification in the notions of poetic license and the power of the solitary genius, I want instead to turn to the field of architectural production itself, using one building as a means of exploring how power relations in society are reproduced in architecture, and also some of the mechanisms that ensure their reproduction.[1]

The building I want to discuss is the Knickerbocker, located in the Bushwick district of Brooklyn, New York. Largely abandoned after riots in 1978, the neighborhood has since become a mecca for African Americans and immigrants, many from the Caribbean, particularly the Dominican Republic. Lacking the relative wealth and middle-class NIMBY clout of Queens, Brooklyn today has more than its share of low-cost housing of various types, of which the Knickerbocker is merely among the most recent.

165

Completed in 1995 and designed by Architrope, a small New York firm, the Knickerbocker Residence is a single-room-occupancy project for homeless and mentally ill veterans. With apartments for forty-four individuals and four couples, it contains facilities for a range of services, including a clinic for the supervision of medications, a common dining room, and even a library. Each apartment has a private bath, kitchenette, and furniture designed by the architects; ceilings are one-half foot higher than the eight-foot standard. Although small, the units radiate warmth and light.

From interior to exterior, the Knickerbocker is of unusual quality, far more than could be expected at $117 per square foot. Principal designer Jonathan Kirschenfeld of Architrope avoided anything that looked remotely institutional, and instead inserted the structure into the neighborhood as a typical brick apartment building, referring to that typology without being limited by it. A townhouse-type unit projecting out from the center of the facade emphasizes its residential character; the finely detailed brickwork with eight-inch brick returns and handsome white precast concrete lintels and sills at the windows give it a decidedly upscale aura. Kirschenfeld managed to transform every obstacle or problem into a positive result. In short, the architecture lends dignity to a building type that too often lacks it, and does so despite a modest budget and uncommonly complicated code requirements.

Knickerbocker Avenue Elevation, Brooklyn, New York. Photograph by Paul Warchol.

Kirschenfeld followed the standard practice of offices that want to draw attention to their work: he sent the project to the major magazines. *Architecture, Architectural Record,* and *Progressive Architecture* each noted it briefly (in a page or less) as an example of worthy social design and little more; it was mentioned in the *New York Times* Real Estate Section.[2] Kirschenfeld also sought to interest New York's most prominent architecture critics, Paul Goldberger and Herbert Muschamp, hoping they would cover the project more extensively in the *Times.* Both ignored the building entirely, and Goldberger remarked to Kirschenfeld, memorably, that he was currently involved more in "cultural" than in architectural criticism.

What "cultural criticism" precisely has occupied Goldberger of late? For one, he was among a group of prestigious architects and critics convened by Peter Eisenman in fall 1996 for the opening of his Aronoff Center for Design and Art at the University of Cincinnati, coincidentally during the same ten-day period when the Knickerbocker officially opened. The videotape of the event, an edited version of which was broadcast on *The Charlie Rose Show,* is hilarious; it is a full-court display of the rituals associated with the cult of art and artists. This gathering of architectural luminaries was clearly intended to certify the building's merit. That "greatness" can be in significant measure associated with circles of class and friendship was clarified by Goldberger when he remarked that the group had assembled at least partly because they are "Peter's friends." As famous architects, deans, and critics, they lent some of their cultural status to the building and its architect.

Viewing displays of elitism and self-proclaimed superiority such as this event, members of the audience rarely possess the knowledge that would enable them to recognize that the cultural status of the work, or the designer, is ultimately arbitrary and chiefly a reflection of the extent to which authorities invest their cultural capital in certain objects. And, of course, the authorities' conferral of status on this building largely reinforces their own status and values as a self-proclaimed elite.

To what values do they subscribe? At the Aronoff event, what was most striking about many of the comments was the contempt they conveyed for the audience. Eisenman, for instance, referred to Walter Benjamin as a "German philosopher unknown to most of you in the audience." Sanford Kwinter remarked that the "interesting people, the intellectuals, admire [the] building." David Childs asserted that it was "good" that taxi drivers in Cincinnati found it hard to find the building's front door. Making it difficult for ordinary people to find the front door, asserted Eisenman, would counter the "sedentary culture" by "bring[ing] the body back into the mind-eye relationship." Beyond this underestimation of "ordinary" people, the values expressed collectively and individually by this group often seemed clichés. They want to "shake things up," to make "another kind of home," to "bring down classicism," and to "embrace infrastructural-scale architectural thought." What *is* remarkable, given the vacuity and even incoherence of much of the discussion, is that such groups have been able to convince so many of their cultural superiority. Entry into this charmed circle is obviously not based primarily on any objective measure of quality, either of thought or work. Most significantly, this group excludes that which does not fit—which returns us to Goldberger's lack of interest in the Knickerbocker: it did not "fit" the concerns of "culture."

By conventional expectations, this building should have received attention: not only was it built on time and under budget, it achieves skillful and subtle resolutions of its many contextual, functional, economic, and social issues, and thus, in every important aspect, it provides a model for other attempts to design SRO housing for diverse groups. Moreover, the partners of Architrope, Andrew Bartle and Jonathan Kirschenfeld, enjoy the kinds of connections that often guarantee recognition. Both received graduate degrees in architecture from Princeton, both spent a year or so at the Institute for Architecture and Urban Studies in the 1970s, and both occasionally teach studios at major northeastern universities. Architrope was a finalist for the prestigious Palladio Prize in 1991, and the firm won New York Art Commission awards in 1993 and 1996, and a Distinguished Architecture Citation from the New York City AIA in 1991. So how can we account for the relative obscurity of this building? The forces at work within any field of cultural production are complicated and twine together in markedly different ways in individual cases. Without a far larger study, it is not possible to make convincing generalizations. And yet, I do think that there are key points to make here about the politics of recognition in architecture, and I want to approach them by offering an example from another part of the cultural world—movies.

In May 1986, I saw a movie that I regard as one of the best of the 1980s. *At Close Range* seemed to have everything that would make it a hit: excellent cast (including Sean Penn and Christopher Walken), compelling story based on real events, strong cinematography, and even a successful title song recorded by Madonna.[3] Yet the movie was withdrawn from release after a few weeks. No critic came forward to champion it; the film dropped from view, neither a popular nor a critical success.

That the movie would disappear was obvious the first time I saw it (sensing this, I saw it two more times), but I have puzzled long on the reasons. Perhaps, given its basis in real life, the pain and horror of the story were simply too devastating, much more so than in the mock thrillers or sensationalized bloodbaths of standard multiplex fare. Moreover, the director did not attempt to psychoanalyze the protagonists or to "explain" their behavior, thereby adding to the shock of the final scenes. Walken's character was the very personification of Hannah Arendt's "banality of evil."

Still, American moviegoers rarely reject a film on the grounds of too much violence. I believe that this film faded from view because its drama takes place in the working class. Further, this working class has none of the stylized phoniness of David Mamet's characters nor the angst-driven moodiness of Sam Peckinpah's. Unflinchingly and unsentimentally, the film depicts the cocky behavior of some unendearing young men whose petty crimes seem to them simply pranks, and who are drawn into a more complex, deeply criminal world whose true nature eludes them until the very end. You will be thinking of other movies in which protagonists succumb to evil, but that is precisely the point. In most movies such protagonists are middle-class or, even better, upper-class; thus, their fall is dramatically satisfying because they have plunged from the heights. In such movies audiences find characters with whom to identify. *At Close Range,* with its unfetishized working-class men and women, offers no such opportunities for comfortable identification.

The parallels to the Knickerbocker Residence are obvious, as is the list of "negative prestige" factors working against this fine building. Its Bushwick location is no doubt the first negative prestige point, but the fact that it is designed for the lowest-level social groups and hence clients possible in our society—the working class, the homeless, and mentally ill veterans—sealed the Knickerbocker Residence's obscurity. *How* to address the needs of low-status populations is a profoundly uncomfortable question not only for the architectural profession but for society as a whole. Both the homeless and mentally ill are stigmatized in contemporary America; misunderstood, demonized, and marginalized, neither group is allowed to participate fully in our society. Communities do not invite social service agencies to develop programs for these groups, nor do they encourage the construction of appropriate facilities in their neighborhoods.

To the world of architecture as currently constituted, such client groups and their invariably downscale districts are not worth lionizing in order to cultivate them for future work, nor are the not-for-profit groups that typically fund and operate such enterprises. At its core, architecture today is supremely elitist, drawing most private and public commissions from various elite groups. Due to their political and social aspirations, many leading American practitioners—Gehry, Eisenman, Graves, Pei, Pelli, Meier, and others—do not invest their prestige, their symbolic capital, in projects for the homeless or the mentally ill; their professional purpose is to address the taste culture of very different segments of the population. To design such facilities therefore transgresses the fundamental premises of Architecture with a capital A. And even if some enlightened practitioners see a certain nobility in such projects, there is certainly little attendant fame. Architects who primarily design low-cost or SRO housing are acknowledged as socially responsible but are never invited into the star hierarchy—nor are their buildings. Although I reject the notion that a museum or library is inherently a more valuable project than an SRO, I want to draw attention to the widespread disinterest in challenging the hierarchy of professional architectural values that ranks housing for the poor and ill among the least desirable kinds of commission. I understand too that this valuation is not an innocent act: as a mechanism for the reproduction of the power of the privileged, it operates also to deny architectural resources (among other resources) to less privileged groups. Need I add that this attitude is primarily responsible for the fact that the architectural profession is now, at the end of the twentieth century, largely superfluous in efforts to find solutions to some of our society's most urgent problems?

1997

Notes

1. The theorist who has most persuasively explored these issues is Pierre Bourdieu, especially in *Distinction: A Social Critique of Taste* (Cambridge, Mass.: Harvard University Press, 1984); but also in "The Forms of Capital,"

in *Handbook of Theory and Research for the Sociology of Education,* ed. J. G. Richardson (New York: Greenwood Press, 1986), 241–58; and *The Logic of Practice* (Cambridge: Polity Press, 1990).

2. *Progressive Architecture,* August 1992, 76; *Architecture,* January 1993, 91; *Architectural Record,* January 1996, 92; "Housing in Brooklyn for Mentally Ill Veterans," Real Estate Section, *New York Times,* September 24, 1995.

3. *At Close Range* (1986), directed by James Foley.

Contributors

John Beardsley is a senior lecturer in landscape architecture at the Harvard Design School. He is the author of several books on art in the great outdoors, including *Earthworks and Beyond* and *Gardens of Revelation.*

Michael Benedikt is director of the Center for American Architecture and Design and the graduate program in interdisciplinary studies at the University of Texas at Austin. He is the author of *Deconstructing the Kimbell* and *For an Architecture of Reality,* and author and editor of *Cyberspace: First Steps.*

Tim Culvahouse is adjunct professor at California College of the Arts, editor of *arcCA* (the quarterly journal of the AIA California Council), and principal of Culvahouse Consulting Group.

Lisa Findley is an architectural journalist and associate professor at the California College of the Arts, where she directs the Master of Architecture program.

Kurt W. Forster is professor of the history of art and architecture at the Bauhaus-Universität, Weimar, Germany. His recent publications include a monograph on the work of Frank O. Gehry, coauthored with Francesco Dal Co.

Kenneth Frampton is Ware Professor of Architecture at the Graduate School of Architecture, Planning, and Preservation at Columbia University. He is the author of many books, including *Le Corbusier: Architect of the Twentieth Century*.

Diane Ghirardo is professor of architecture and art history at the University of Southern California. She is the author of *Architecture after Modernism*.

Charles Jencks, writer and designer in London, is the author of many books, including, most recently, *The Iconic Building: The Power of Enigma*.

David Leatherbarrow is professor of architecture at the University of Pennsylvania. His most recent book is *Topographical Stories: Studies in Landscape and Architecture*.

Nancy Levinson is the former associate editor and coeditor of *Harvard Design Magazine*. She is now director of the Phoenix Urban Research Laboratory, writes "Pixel Points" for ArtsJournal.com, and is a contributor to *Architectural Record* and other magazines.

Hélène Lipstadt is a cultural historian. She has taught at the Université of Montreal and the Massachusetts Institute of Technology. She is a regional editor of *The Journal of Architecture,* a founding director of DOCOMOMO US, and the author of a forthcoming book on the relationship of Pierre Bourdieu and Erwin Panofsky.

Juhani Pallasmaa is a practicing architect and professor of architecture at the Helsinki University of Technology. He is the author of several books, including *Eyes of the Skin: Architecture and the Senses*.

Timothy M. Rohan is assistant professor in the art history program at the University of Massachusetts, Amherst. His research concentrates on postwar architecture, urbanism, and theory. He is working on a study of Paul Rudolph and has published articles in *Grey Room, Casabella,* and *Architectural Design*.

William S. Saunders is editor of *Harvard Design Magazine* and of the Harvard Design Magazine Readers. He is the author of *Modern Architecture: Photography by Ezra Stoller.*

Roger Scruton is an English philosopher, essayist, foxhunter, farmer, composer, man of letters, and author of more than twenty books, including *The Aesthetics of Architecture* and *The Classical Vernacular.*

Daniel Willis is department head and professor of architecture at Pennsylvania State University. He is the author of *The Emerald City and Other Essays on the Architectural Imagination.*